Acknowledgements

Avo-Megger UK, for their kind permission to use photographs of their test equipment throughout this publication.
Jim McCall. One of my early tutors when I first started out in the industry. When I started teaching more recently, he again mentored me, mainly because he owned the training business where I work!
Mark Parsey. Another major influence on my life. As a friend and employee I have spent the majority of my working life with him. Through him I have gained great experience of contracting in all spheres of electrical work, including more recently, the teaching business.
David Gee for his final excellent editing and artwork. And finally, a big thank you to the following for their help and assistance. Judy Dunham and Jill Bamber for their help and support around the office.
And too many friends and family to list. You know who you are.

Disclaimer

While I believe that all the information in this work is correct, a person must rely on his or her own skill and judgement while using it. I do not accept any liability for any loss due to my errors or omissions. Where any reference is made to legislation, it cannot be assumed to be legal advice, as I am not a lawyer! Being a realist though, I would be thankful for input from purchasers regarding small errors, potential improvements or differing opinion. The author can be contacted via the address below.

Published by:

Electrickery Publishing
JM Training Consultants Ltd.
Tameside House,
Tameside Business Centre,
Windmill Lane,
Denton,
Manchester M34 3QS.

Copyright

This work is covered under the Berne Convention 2003 and Universal Copyright Convention. All rights are reserved. This work may not be reproduced, stored or transmitted by any means, unless you have written permission from the author.

© 2007 Alan Lynch

Contents

Introduction...

Having worked in the electrical industry for over twenty years as a "sparky" and more recently as a lecturer, certain things have gradually dawned on me. I had always known how standards of training and installation could have been better amongst my peers, but the question is "How do you achieve this?

I was very lucky in my early years. I served my time as an indentured apprentice with one of the old regional electricity boards. The training was second to none but I did not realise this at the time! When I started teaching, being a little rusty from the classroom, I sat and read what was around on the market. What I found reminded me that nothing has changed much in my time in the industry. Installation books are written by very educated people who don't do installation work for a living. The publications are technically correct but lacking in real-life problem solving. They are also written in "exact" language, which is difficult for the contracting electrician to follow, never mind be interested in! I always read a book at college and half understood it. Only when I discussed it with a wise old electrician who explained it in plain English, did I "get it". This was the beginning of the idea to write my own book.

The final catalyst to get this started has been the inclusion of the IEE electrical regulations into the building regulations in England and Wales, more commonly known as "Part P". This has mainly affected the kitchen and bathroom fitters, who now have to comply with the law when doing electrical installation work as a sideline to their main job. Within the electrical industry is a lot of hostility to these chaps being "legitimised" by doing short domestic installer courses. The time served man regards these individuals as "5 day wonders".

They scoff, *"How can these guys become electricians in one week?"*

Well, I am one of those trainers who look after these people. I know I cannot turn out "electricians" in a week. However, the law of the land says a person must be competent to work on an electrical system and I can teach a person that much with no problems. At the very least, I give them what they need to get started for a new, law abiding and safe career as domestic electricians. Besides this, it is a pleasure to see a student coming through my door as keen as mustard with a brand new test meter under his arm saying, "Show me how it all works!" This to me is like a breath of fresh air!

You may be asking now, *"How does he do this?"* Well, the answer is easy.

Simply, I have an in-depth understanding of regulations and installation science. This can sometimes be unnecessarily deep concerning the "domestic" installation. With this in mind, I can strip away all the big words and technical language and give it to the student in layman's terms. In addition, because I am a practicing electrician I can also bust all the electrical myths and give tips for making the job easier and quicker.

This book is run in the general format of a five-day "domestic installer course." All the diagrams and explanations are just as I teach in class. I have also based this publication around an actual new build bungalow, so you will see the whole Part P process unfold before you. I have photographed all steps with accompanying explanations. This will be the secret to you grasping the world of legal and safe domestic installation.

To summarise, this work is mainly for kitchen and bathroom fitters, who "spark" as a by-product of their main job. However, it will be useful for craft apprentices, central heating engineers, self-confessed "rusty" electricians and even keen DIYers!

Remember to read a little at a time, as you don't want to become swamped. When training I have plenty of tea and smoke breaks, not for my benefit of course, but to allow the student to recover and reflect!

In this book, you will have to refer to other publications as you read. The ones required are "BS 7671" and the IEE "On Site Guide" (OSG from now on!). I will mainly refer to the OSG as it is more Part P friendly and you will be familiar with it after your 5-day wonder course! Within the text, all page referrals such as **(p12)** refer to this book. All referrals to other books will be stated as such **(p12 OSG)**. As you refer to these other publications, it will be handy to have a highlighter pen handy, just like we do in class!

Finally, I must say that this book cannot be a substitute for training. Even though this book follows in detail a "domestic installer" course, it must be used in conjunction with good personal training. It would be fair to say that reading and understanding this work will put you in the position of "fore warned is fore armed."

I have enjoyed my career as an electrician and teacher. Being an author is a new venture for me and though difficult at times, has been a very satisfying experience. I do hope you enjoy reading this as much as I did putting it together.

Alan Lynch
January 2007

OK, so you have a domestic electrical job to do and nowadays you need to comply with Part P of the building regulations to comply with the law. The first thing you need to do is work out the route you are going to take to deal with this. Basically, to comply you have two options....

1 Self certification scheme membership
2 Notification directly to the local building control

Option 1 is pricey to join but for the regular electrical dabbler is the only way to go. You have to join one of the present five self-certification schemes that are approved by the government. You satisfy their competence criteria and are then allowed to do the work and self certify it. You then inform the scheme provider where you have been working and what you have been up to with a small cost per job of around a couple of pounds. They then inform the local building control people who issue a building compliance certificate. The only down side, as stated, is the annual membership which runs to many hundreds of pounds per annum.

Option 2 is the route to go for very occasional electrical work or DIY work. In this instance, you contact your local building control to inform them that you intend to work on a job. They usually post out a form to find out what you are doing and then monitor the job to make sure it complies with building regulations. The cost of this is usually a sliding scale depending on the contract price, but you are looking at around £80 per job minimum (At time of writing). When they are satisfied that all is well with the job, they will then issue a building compliance certificate. If you are doing a kitchen extension or other large job, then the notification and fee will cover all the building work including the electrical part.

Next, we have to look at what is notifiable. This covers mostly everything! Your local building control will advise accordingly. Below is a list, which covers most:

Notifiable:

- Rewires
- New single circuits added to an existing installation
- Minor work in kitchens and bathrooms
- Most outdoor works

Non-notifiable:

- Minor work not in a bathroom or kitchen
- Swapping sockets, switches or any accessories
- Rewiring damaged circuits (as long as it is done in the same cable and route of the original circuit)
- Installation earthing upgrades

Whether or not the works are notifiable they are still covered by Part P of the building regulations and so to comply:

All work must be tested and a certificate issued!

The main purpose of this book is to:

- Assist a person to comply with Part P of the building regulations.
- Scupper myths that exist within the electrical industry.

As the myths are busted, you will see them in red type. To put you at ease then, I shall kick off with the first one:

MYTH   *Electrical work is "HARD" or "ELITE".*

You may be a little surprised by this, but trust me, all will be revealed. When one breaks down each part of the procedure, it is actually very simple and bordering on common sense! To comply with Part P of the building regulations you could get the document and trawl through it for a long time. All you really need to know is that to comply with the law Part P, you only need comply with BS7671. The old name for this publication is presently the 16th edition of the wiring regulations. In effect, you have to:

- DESIGN the installation, so it is safe
- INSTALL the wiring and accessories to the standard
- INSPECT and TEST your new work for compliance
- CERTIFICATE the work you have completed

It can be seen then, that in reality Part P has been a "storm in a teacup" so to speak. That is if all electrical operatives have been doing their work properly! For the electrician, it is easy – test it and leave a certificate! Sadly, this part of the job is among the most neglected. Therefore, the next myth to be busted is;

MYTH   *Electricians test properly, everyone else do not know how to!*

Remember, I have been "on the tools" for years. I know what happens on the job. The truth of the matter is that most electricians do not test properly and some do not test anything at all! "A sweeping statement", I may here you mutter, but true none the less. It is probably another reason why so many domestic "electricians" are very anti- Part P. They will be exposed as incompetent as their flawed or absent paperwork will always "catch" them out. At the time of writing, the prosecutions have begun so all this should be borne out in due course.

Before we get on to the work you are going to be doing, it is important to get some basics out of the way. You need to know these items because some of the terms are mentioned on an Electrical Installation Certificate. (EIC). To comply with Part P you will have to fill out these certificates. I shall cover each of these one-step at a time. To summarise you shall cover the following topics:

- Ohms law
- Power triangle
- Earthing terminology
- Earthing systems
- Exposed and extraneous conductive parts
- Direct and indirect contact
- SELV
- Class I, II and III equipment
- Overcurrent protective device types and disconnection times

Ohms law

This "law" is the cornerstone of the electrical world. It is the statement of the relationship between electrical voltage, current and resistance. You may be surprised to learn that if you can grasp Ohm's law, then you have got about as technical in the world of electrickery as you can get! Referring to the triangles you can see the four values V, I, R and Z:

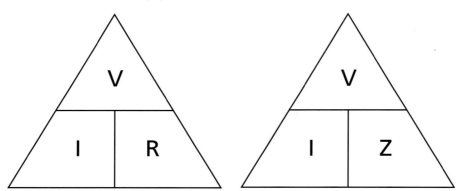

The key to these values, units and symbols are:

Symbol	V	I	R	Z
Meaning	Electrical "pressure"	Electrical "current"	Electrical "resistance"	Electrical "impedance"
Unit used	Volt	Amp	Ohm	Ohm
Unit abbreviation	V	A	Ω	Ω

The easiest way to figure all this out is to compare an electrical circuit to a garden hosepipe:

- When you turn on the water to the hose, the system will stabilise to a steady flow.
- The pressure is constant and a set current is flowing.
- The flow is governed by the bore resistance or impedance of the pipe AND the pressure pushing the water along.

If you crimp the pipe, the water will slow down. This is because the resistance or impedance of the pipe has just increased. To get the same current flowing again you have two choices:

- Turn up the pressure to increase the flow.
- Decrease the resistance/impedance by removing the obstruction of the pipe.

And so, it is more or less the same with an electrical circuit.

Looking again at the triangles please do not start fretting with the complication of the terms "resistance" and "impedance" (The science for this is outside your scope but basically resistance is a d.c. or direct current value and impedance is an a.c. or alternating current value. If you are not familiar with this terminology, go to the glossary at the back of this book). Now the good news for you is that on your installations the values are so close they are not considered different, so therefore, for you, *they are one and the same!*

To clarify now, these values are linked by the law. If you know **two** of these values then you can easily find the **third**. You do this by placing your hand over the value you **do not know** on the triangle. You can find the solution by doing the resultant sum with the other two known values. The six sums that can be found using these two equations are:

- **V=IxR or V=IxZ**
- **I=V/R or I=V/Z**
- **R=V/I or Z=V/I**

It is now a good time to do a few examples, so you get to know your way around the law. When you look at these diagrams that follow, you will see this symbol. ⊣▢⊢ It is the symbol for an electrical resistance or loading. It could therefore be a table light, an immersion heater or a shopping centre!

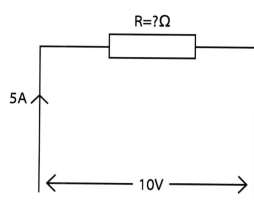

- V=10V, I= 5A, R=?Ω

Answer: R=V/I
           R=10/5=**2Ω**

- V=100V, I=?A, Z= 1000Ω

    Answer: I=V/Z
            I= 100/1000=**0.1A**

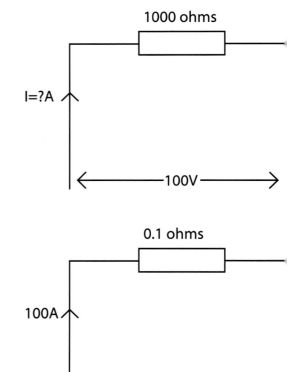

1000 ohms

I=?A

—100V—

- V=?V, I= 100A, R= 0.1Ω

    Answer: V=IxR
            V=100x0.1=**10V**

0.1 ohms

100A

—V=?V—

So there the lesson ends and you may say,

"So what has all this got to do with wiring a kitchen then?"

To illustrate the workings of the law, we shall now do a "real life" example:
Let's take a cooker circuit that you are to install. You are going to pop this circuit on a 30A rewireable fuse (BS 3036) (If you are not sure what one of these is, there is a picture and explanation on **p30**.)
In the event of a fault, you need, as a competent person, to be sure that the fuse will blow, so no one is electrocuted or the property burns down. Now go to the **OSG p6** where you shall see the list of this book's appendices. In this list, you should spot **appendix 2.** It is titled,

"Maximum permissible measured earth fault loop *impedance*."

If you go to the table indicated on **OSG p89** you should find two tables for a BS 3036 fuse rated at 30A. One is for 0.4 second maximum disconnection and one is for 5 second maximum disconnection. Disconnection times are covered later in this section but all you need to know is that the 0.4s maximum disconnection time   is for socket outlet circuits and the maximum disconnection time of 5s is for everything else (on domestic installs anyhow). So if our cooker were to use a plain switch it would be a 5s circuit or if the cooker unit had a socket outlet fitted then it would be 0.4s circuit. Also, we will wire the cooker in 6mm² twin and earth cable which has a 2.5mm² protective conductor. This gets us to figures now! You should find:

- 0.91Ω for 0.4second and 2.21Ω for 5-second disconnection.

Now we have impedance figures and we have a voltage of 240V. We can now do the maths for both. Please refer to the triangles on **p10**.

- 5 sec disconnection calculation (Max Z=2.21Ω)
  I =?A, V=240V, Z=2.21Ω
  I=V/Z
  I=240/2.21= **109A**

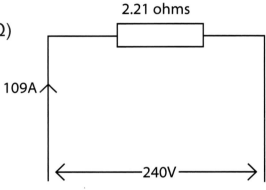

- 0.4 sec disconnection calculation   Max Z=0.91Ω
  I=?A, V=240V, Z=0.91Ω
  I=V/Z
  I=240/0.91=**264A**

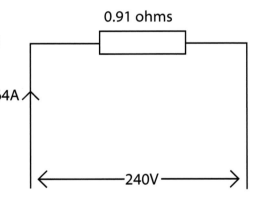

So in the example given,
109A flowing through a 30A fuse will blow it in 5 seconds or
264A flowing through a 30A fuse will blow it in it 0.4 seconds.

To tie this in with Ohms law then, on our examples the voltage is fixed:

- So as the impedance goes down the current flow goes up, and vice versa.
- The higher the current, the quicker the fuse will "blow."

Luckily for you budding electricians, there is an instrument that is called, not surprisingly, an "earth loop impedance tester" which will take the measurement for you directly. This exercise has been only to demonstrate Ohms law in action!

The power triangle

Following on from the above, we now come to another triangle, which works in exactly the same fashion but now we have new terms.

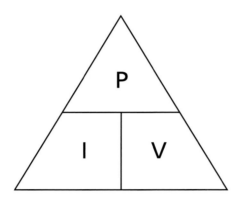

The key to these values, units and symbols are:

Symbol	P	I	V
Meaning	Electrical "power"	Electrical "current"	Electrical "voltage"
Unit used	Watt	Amp	Volt
Unit abbreviation	W	A	V

This one is a lot easier to picture than Ohms law. Power is the product of a current flowing in something and the voltage applied to it. Again, if you have two of the values you can easily work out the third. This is done once again by placing your hand over the value you need. This will give us three equations:

P=IxV
I=P/V
V=P/I

This time the middle equation you *will* use on a regular basis. When you propose to install a circuit, you need to know how many amps you are to use from the supply. This will dictate the size of cable and fuse/breaker you install. The problem is that nothing you buy is marked in "amps", it always comes marked with "watts". Before we do a few examples, one thing that needs looking at is the watt. It is a very small amount of power so a lot of equipment is marked in kW, which means 1000's of watts. It just saves many zeros on information leaflets! Now we will look at a couple of power calculation examples.

I-ON

- P= 4kW, I=?A, V= 240V

  Answer: I=P/V
  $$I=4000/240=\textbf{16.7A}$$

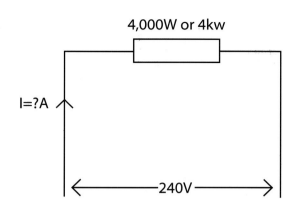

- P=? KW, I=32A, V=240V

  Answer: P=IxV
  $$P= 32x240=7680W=\textbf{7.68kW}$$

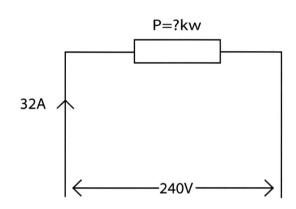

You will find that most electricians don't do a calculator routine on this type of work. 1kW of power at 240V is around 4.2A, so they reckon on around **4A per kW**. Now let me show you a couple of examples of this "ball park" calculation:

A 4kW oven is about 16A (4X4=16A)
A 9.5kW shower would be about 38A. (9x4=36 and 1/2 kW over would be 2A to give us 38A)

Just for fun now, fun?, and to finish off this section let us take a 100W light bulb and supply it with different voltages to see how many amps we would need for the 100W required.

We shall supply our imaginary 100W lamp with voltages of 1V, 100V, and 100,000V:

At 1V the current needed would be I= P/V=100/1= **100A** (huge cable!)
At 100V the current needed would be I= P/V= 100/100= **1A** (little cable)
At 100,000V the current needed would be I= P/V= 100/100,000= **0.001A** (tiny cable!)

This illustrates the reason why when you go for a picnic with your family in the countryside you will see pylons everywhere. They are marked "DANGER OF DEATH" 132,000V, 275,000V, or even 400,000V. As you have seen above, power is a product of voltage and current, so you have two routes to get the electrical energy required across the land:

- Big current with low voltage or
- Small current with high voltage

The power companies obviously have to shift the maximum power with the smallest cables possible and thus crank up the voltage as high as possible. It then has to be transformed down to a safer level once it reaches your home, as 400,000V would not work very well. The main problem being that a spark could perhaps jump 15 feet across your living room to greet you!

You may have noticed that I have used 240V in my sums above when you may note that the voltage mentioned in books is 230V. To comply with European harmonization the declared voltage is:

- **230V +or – 10%.**

This gives us a scope of 207- 253 V.
Our supply is in reality still 240V but *declared* at 230V. Sums, however, are still done with 240V because that is what it really is!

Earthing terminology

It is quite important that the Part P electrician knows his earthing terminology properly as it is noted on the paperwork. And if the person goes for accreditation from one of the scheme providers, he must know the names of the various terms to satisfy his inspector. The terms and pictures are in your **OSG p 27-29**, but just to reiterate there are only five. Do not worry about the reasons for earthing, for now, just get to know the terms! This is exactly as I draw it on the board in class

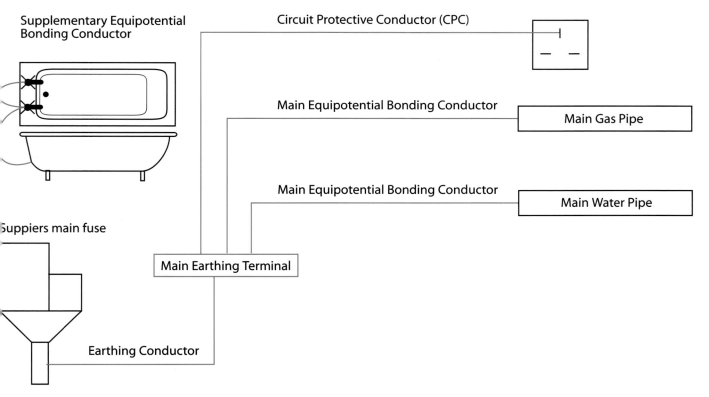

Supplementary Equipotential Bonding Conductor

Circuit Protective Conductor (CPC)

Main Equipotential Bonding Conductor

Main Gas Pipe

Main Equipotential Bonding Conductor

Main Water Pipe

Suppiers main fuse

Main Earthing Terminal

Earthing Conductor

Earthing conductor

This is the last route out of a house, for the current, in the event of an earth fault. This is some times wrongly called the "main earth" or even "main bonding". A house has only one earthing conductor. Here you can see the earthing conductor coming from the electricity company main fuse unit. OSG tells you what size you need, usually a 16mm² cable.

Main Earthing Terminal

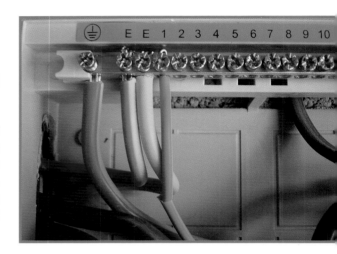

This is the name of the terminal, to which the earthing conductor described previously, is connected.

The term "main earthing terminal" is usually shortened to "met". It can either be external to the consumer unit, (as on the previous page), or within a consumer unit as shown in the adjacent picture. Either is fine. This is the project bungalow met. The incoming earthing conductor is the biggest cable on the left.

Main equipotential bonding conductor

This cable, within the domestic install, connects the main incoming services such as the gas and water to the main earthing terminal. The usual size is 10mm^2. Here you can see a connection to the mains water incomer via an earth clamp.

Supplementary equipotential bonding conductor

This conductor is a protective earthing cable that connects metalwork and equipment together. It is usually seen in bathrooms or under kitchen sinks. These conductors are used in varying sizes in the electrical industry but for the domestic job, the only one used is 4mm^2. Bathroom bonding is covered in detail in **Part 6, special locations**, further on in this book.

Circuit protective conductor

This is the official name for the earth wire that accompanies a circuit from the met to its destination. It is abbreviated to "cpc". A cpc comes in many shapes and sizes in the electrical world, but on domestic work you will generally find it within the sheath of twin and earth cabling. When you install twin and earth cable you may be aware that the cpc is sometimes smaller than the live and neutral. In the interest of completion I shall list them for you.

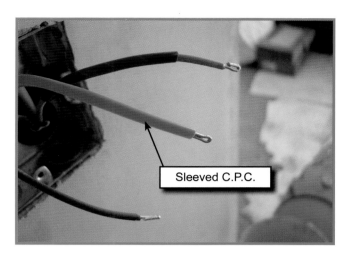
Sleeved C.P.C.

LIVE AND NEUTRAL CONDUCTOR OF TWIN AND EARTH CABLE.	ASSOCIATED CPC.
1.0mm²	1.0mm²
1.5mm²	1.0mm²
2.5mm²	1.5mm²
4.0mm²	1.5mm²
6.0mm²	2.5mm²
10mm²	4.0mm²
16mm²	6.0mm²

Earthing systems

As we have seen previously, to comply with Part P, and the law, we need only test and supply an Electrical Installation Certificate. This is usually abbreviated to E.I.C. On this form, you have to record the type of earthing system that supplies the premises. If you were to look in the definitions of BS 7671, a system is defined as:

- *"A single source of energy and an installation."*

I will define it now a little simpler to help you remember:

- ***"From the sub-station to your play station!"***

I-ON

In other words, the system is from the sub-station in the street, into your house, through your concealed wiring, and ending at your lights and sockets. The sub-station is the thing you walk past on the way home from the pub at night that "hums!" It is a great big transformer and is the final destination of the electricity from the power station network.

The electricity supplier then has to get this supply from the sub-station to your house. We shall now examine the different ways, of which there are three. Please do not worry about the letters, you need only know what I am about to tell you, so read on....

- *On all the diagrams that follow, the left of the dotted line is the street supply side & to the right is the property installation. Also brown, blue and green are live, neutral and earth respectively.*

TN-S system

If you go to work at a property that was built before the late 1960's, then it will probably be fed via an old fashioned oiled paper insulated and lead sheathed supply cable. This is known in power company lingo as a PILC (paper insulated lead sheath) logically enough! The live and neutral go up the middle of the cable and the outer sheath is earth. Today this known as a TN-S system. If you look at my schematic and the following photo, you will see that the easy way to remember the name of this system is that a TN-**S** supply has a

SEPARATE EARTH AND NEUTRAL ALL THE WAY THROUGH STREET AND PROPERTY

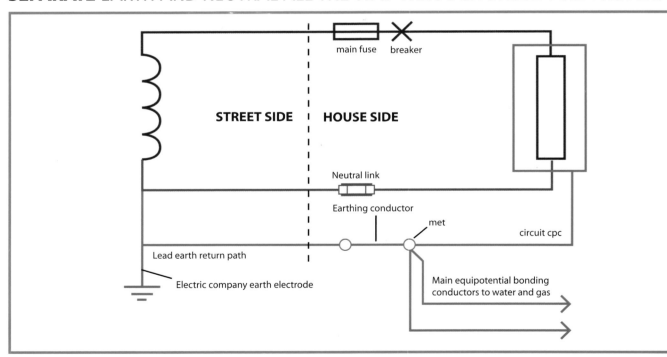

Looking at the diagram, the supply transformer at the sub-station, (that's the coil thing on the left of the drawing) feeds a separate live, neutral and earth to the property.

This is what it would look like in real life! An old paper insulated, lead sheathed cable is terminating into a main fuse unit. The lead sheath is the earth back to the supply tranformer. You can see an earth clamp fitted to the lead sheath. From this then an earthing conductor leads to a not very straight main earthing terminal! The terminal is hiding behind the red and black meter tails. The neutral link is the little black box next to the main fuse. This is a very old supply but it has had the old main fuse replaced by a more up to date model some time in the recent past. This main fuse would have started out as an open wire fuse in days gone by.

TN-C-S system

By the late 1960's the electricity companies looked at the old fashioned TN-S and decided to change the supply delivery. Their reasoning to change was mainly cost. If you look at the TN-S system above you see that the neutral and earth end up at the same place at the supply transformer. They decided to combine both jobs in one wire. In the beginning the system was known as "PME". This stood for Protective Multiple Earthing. These "multiple" earths can be seen on my diagram, earthing the combined neutral-earth on the street side of the supply. Again looking at my schematic and the following photo you will noot that the easy way to remember the meaning of this system is that a TN-**C-S** system has a

COMBINED EARTH AND NEUTRAL ON SUPPLY SIDE AND A **SEPARATE** EARTH AND NEUTRAL ON INSTALLATION SIDE.

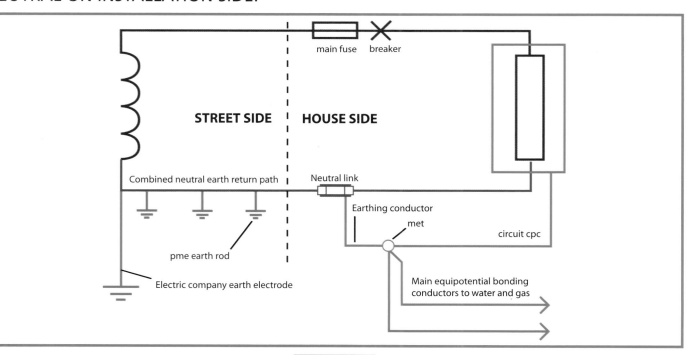

On my schematic on the previous page, you will notice that the earthing conductor is connected to the incoming combined neutral-earth.

This is a "real life" TN-C-S install. The supply cable comes into the main fuse at the bottom, just out of the picture. Refering again to the diagram above it is now a two core supply cable. Remember though, one of these cores is doing two jobs now. It is a neutral AND an earth. The neutral (black cable) coming from the top side of the unit has a link inside through to the visible earth point . This is where the neutral and earth now become separate conductors. From here the earthing conductor goes to the met. Note the power company's "PME" sticker fitted.

T-T system

This system is not used so much, at least in the city where I work! Here the power company supply you with *no earth* at all! On your install you have to drive a rod or "earth electrode" into the ground to get an earth path back to the supply transformer. The "T" stands for terra which is latin for earth. Therefore, if the power company earth their transformer at their end of the system and you drive in a rod at your end, then you have two rods in the earth.....so the easy way to remember **TT**:

TERRA TERRA- EARTH ROD AT THEIR END AND YOURS.

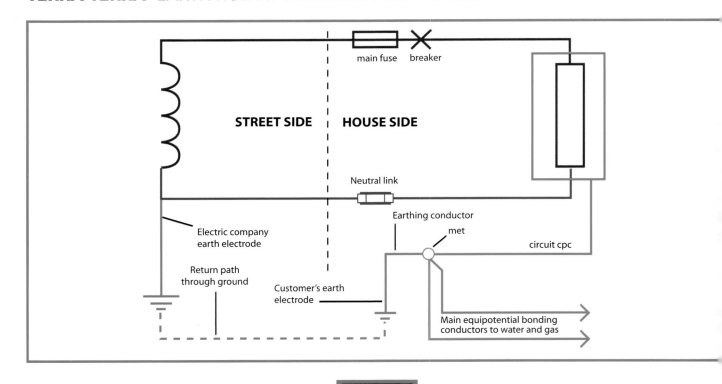

I must appologise now, as I could not find a TT supply at the time of writing. They are rare in the metropolis! If you come across one on your travels, you will know it immediately. From the met the earthing conductor will not go to the main fuse position. It will disappear somewhere outside en- route to the customer's earth electrode.

Just to finish off this section a word of warning. If you go to a TN-S job as at the top of this section, DO NOT fit an earth clamp to the cable sheath if it is broken or damaged. If you squash the power company's supply cable and it blows up, there could be a 1000A breaker protecting it at the sub-station end. It would be one hell of a bang under the stairs with you right in front of it! Even worse DO NOT "convert" the supply to TN-C-S by popping the earthing conductor into the neutral somehow. Please,please phone the local power company! The diagram below illustrates this very clearly!

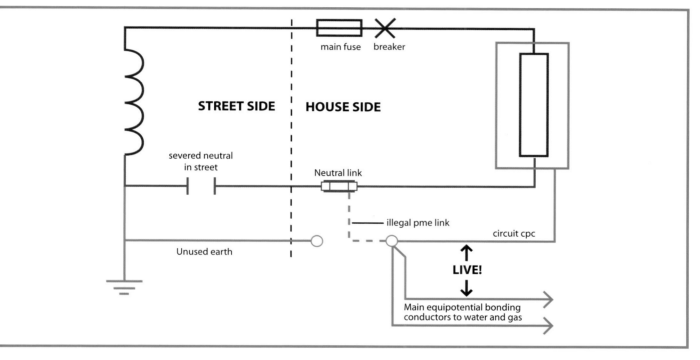

A "cowboy" contractor has "converted" this supply to TN-C-S as the clamp was awkward to get to or broken. Later in time the supply neutral has gone "open circuit" in the street at some point. If you check out this diagram you can follow the live side of the supply through the load and back to the neutral link, this is now gone live as there is no neutral return to the supply transformer. That puts a live supply on to the "illegal" pme link which energizes the main earthing terminal. Therefore, every earth wire connected to the met has become live.

ALL METALWORK IN THE HOUSE IS NOW ENERGIZED!

You may say "Oh yes that looks rare". Not so, burnt out mains cabling in the street is more common than you'd think, so never ever do it! By the way that is why a TN-C-S system is also called pme or protective multiple earthing. Regular joints are earthed out via rods in the ground, check out the TN-C-S drawing previously. If the combined neutral earth severs, then the "pme" rods will carry a little current to limit the voltage on the installation.

Exposed and extraneous conductive parts

These two terms are part of the world of electrical jargon that I would like to cover next and shall be dealt with separately.

- Exposed conductive part.

This is exactly as described, it is a part of an installation which is made from metal and which you can touch! Examples would be a metal consumer-unit or perhaps a lounge chrome dimmer, these items are: exposed, conductive and part of the installation!

- Extraneous conductive part.

This is a part of an installation which is metal, can be touched, but is nothing to do with the installation. Examples would be a gas pipe supplying a boiler or pipework within a bathroom. The easy way to remember is the word "extra" in extraneous. If you rip out the boiler, the lights will still work!

Direct, indirect contact

These are two very important terms. Again I shall describe them one at a time.

Protection against direct contact.

The BS 7671 definition of this is " contact of persons or livestock with live parts" If you open a consumer unit and stick your finger in, you have just demonstated direct contact to yourself! In other words, you stick your finger in expecting an electric shock and would get it! So how do you protect against this contact? The primary methods you use everyday. The cable you buy has insulation fitted to it and when you screw back a socket or put the lid on a consumer unit you introduce barriers and enclosures.
It has to be said that this is common sense but the regulations are written in very specific and legalistic language.

Protection against indirect contact.

In BS 7671 definitions this is listed as " contact with exposed conductive parts which have become live under fault conditions" In this scenario you are leaning against a gas pipe and get a shock off it as a fault has occoured somewhere in the house. This is not good, obviously! BS 7671 lists a number of protection measures against indirect contact. There are others but the only three you will see on your travels are are:

- Earthed equipotential bonding and automatic disconnection of supply (EEBADS)
- Electrical separation
- Class II equipment

We will now look at these separately.

Earthed equipotential bonding and automatic disconnection of supply.
This is a very long winded and technical sounding protection but you do use this everyday at work. Honestly! Simply it is earth wires and fuses.Let us cover each word or phrase, one at a time to help explain the term more fully.

Earthed- you earth metalwork to carry any fault current away.

Equipotential bonding- this term means equal potential or equal voltage. If a live wire fell off the inside of a washing machine a current would flow to earth, so far so good. However while we wait for the fuse to "blow" there would be a voltage on that washing machine. I will make up a voltage of say 100V. Now if the washer case is 100V, then the cpc back to the met will also be at 100V. Consequently then every wire connected to the met will rise to 100V. In effect every bit of "earthed metalwork" in the dwelling goes live to the value of 100V!
You may think it extremely dangerous but actually it is quite safe! The house is in effect an "equipotential zone." This means that all the metalwork in the house is "linked" together at the same voltage .

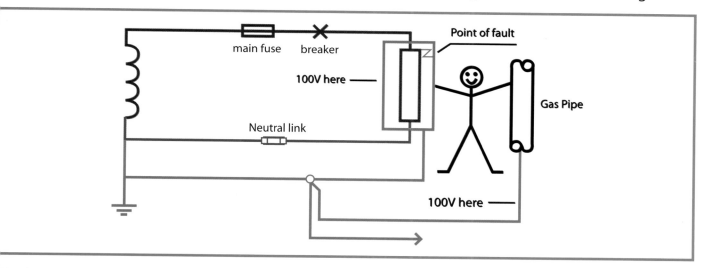

The best way to explain why our "victim" above is still smiling is to talk about the old-fashioned name for voltage. Some people still call voltage "potential difference". What this means is that you have to have a potential or voltage difference across something for a current to flow. If you plug in a table lamp, it lights because you give it a "live" voltage of 240V and a "neutral" voltage of 0V. Therefore the potential difference across the light is:

- 240-0=240V and the light lights up!

Now our "victim" has 100V on one hand and 100V on the other, so the potential difference is now:

- 100-100=0V and he is unaware of any problem!

"It can't be!" I hear you cry. Well it is the same as when you picnic in the countryside. You can look up at those birds on bare overhead power lines. Some of these bare power lines are carrying 400,000V. The creature has 400kV on one leg and 400kV on the other, so the "potential" across him is

- 400,000-400,000=0V hence he keeps tweeting!

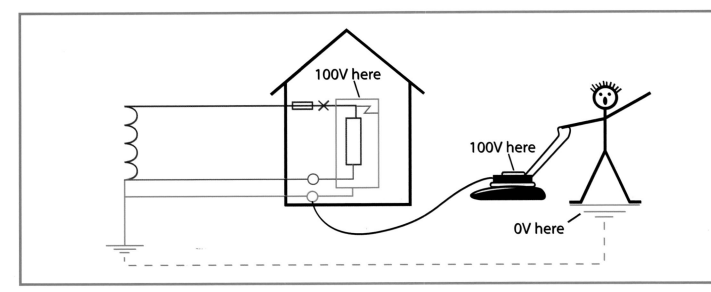

As a post-script to the above, while we wait for the washing machine fuse to "blow" a real "victim" is outside mowing the lawn. Due to equipotential bonding this unfortunate chap now has 100V on his lawnmower. He is also standing on bare ground which has a voltage of 0V. Therefore the "potential difference" across him is:

- 100-0V=100V.

This is really bad news for the gardener, so now you know why you need rcd protection when you take electricity outdoors! Rcds are covered later in the testing section.

Automatic disconnection of supply- This is a fancy name for a fuse or circuit breaker protecting a circuit.

So then, to knit all this together then,
earthed equipotential bonding and automatic disconnection of supply basically means:

- You earth the installation, connect all the metalwork together and put all circuits on a fuse or breaker.
- Luckily for us this term can be abbreviated to EEBADS!

So you see, you have been installing EEBADS as protection against indirect contact for years and not even realised, you clever people!

Electrical separation

The only example of electrical separation you will find in a home is a shaver socket in a bathroom. The reason it is allowed in this part of a house is best described by the following diagrams.

In this example a "victim" is making contact with a live part supplied by a normal earthed supply. He gets a shock due to current flowing through him, to earth and back to the supply. In other words he is completing an electrical circuit.

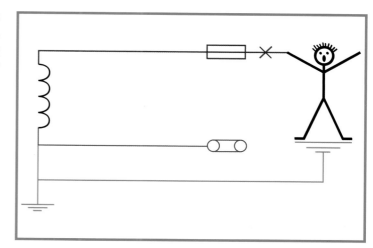

In this example the person is making contact with the output of an "isolation" transformer. That is a shaver socket to you! Even though he is touching one side of the output, he feels nothing, as the circuit is broken to the other side of the output. This is because the secondary is not earthed; it is "electrically separated" from earth. You could now say "Ah but what if he makes contact with the other side of the shaver socket with his other finger" Yes he would get a shock but he would probably deserve it!

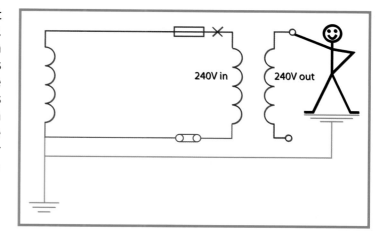

Class II equipment

This is basically any equipment fitted with no earth required. If it is not made of metal you cannot get a shock from it! All classes of equipment are covered further on, within this section, in more detail.

Protection against both direct AND indirect contact(SELV)

This is, in my opinion a strange term, but it is in BS 7671 and also is to be recorded, if fitted, on an Electrical Installation Certificate;

To explain it, you need to know that in the world of Part P and BS7671 there are only two voltages that affect you:

Extra low voltage   less than 50V
Low voltage   50V and above

Do not forget then, next time you get a shock from doing something stupid on a job, it was only a LOW voltage electric shock! Following on from this then BS7671 lists in the home as protection against both direct and indirect contact a new term to be covered, SELV. The full name for this term is:

- Separated extra low voltage.

This then explains what the regulations people are on about:

- It has an electrically separate output, so protection against indirect contact is achieved just like the shaver socket previously.

- The output is extra low voltage so protection against direct contact is achieved (you would not be in danger touching the voltage present).

So now you may wonder about examples of SELV and yes, you fit these items all the time. How about door chime transformers and 12V downlights!

And this is spare and fresh from my car boot! It is a humble extra low votage lighting transformer and here you can see the term "SELV" pointed out .

Class I, II and III equipment

A nice bit of easy terminology here. These three classes you do fit all the time:

Class I   Any equipment with an earth terminal on it.
Class II   Double insulated equipment, no earth fitted.
Class III SELV equipment, no earth fitted.

- Equipment which is Class I usually does not have any mark on it. The earth terminal makes it obvious which class it is.
- Any Class II equipment has a symbol that depicts a square within a square. An example could be a 240V fan with no earth.
- Class III equipment has a diamond on it with a III in the middle, if you're lucky! Again if it carries no mark it is obvious what it is because it will be supplied via a SELV transformer. Just as Class II you do not earth it. (remember it is SELV-electrically *separated* from earth)

Overcurrent protective devices and disconnection times

Overcurrent protective devices

"Overcurrent protective device" is a technical name for a fuse or miniature circuit breaker. It basically does what it says; it protects a circuit cable from an "overcurrent." There are three types of overcurrent:

- Short circuit current. This is what happens if a live and neutral touch.
- Earth fault current. Same as above but here a live is touching earth.
- Overload current. This is a fault that can occur in a "healthy" circuit.
  Perhaps too many appliances plugged into a ring circuit causing a fuse to "blow".

Ok, so far so good. This is straightforward stuff. As a domestic installer, you have to record on an EIC what you have installed to protect your circuit. Therefore, you need to know your fuses and breakers so we will look at them here.

The only four that you will generally see on a domestic installation will be one of these:

- BS 3036, the old type rewireable.
- BS 1361, cartridge type fuse.
- BSEN 60898, miniature circuit breaker.
- BS 3871, miniature circuit breaker.

  You can see some of these in the following pictures.

Before we move on, we need to discuss these devices in a little more detail. As we have seen above, in the Ohm's law section, in the event of a short circuit or earth fault it is possible for many hundreds or even thousands of amps to flow.

I-ON

We have to be sure that the protective device fitted is safely capable of disconnecting the fault without "blowing up" and perhaps causing a fire! On an Electrical Installation Certificate (EIC) you also have to record this "breaking capacity" Go now to **p50 OSG** and all will be revealed.

You should be now looking at table 7.2A. This table tells you how many amps a fuse or breaker will safely disconnect without damage. Looking at our typical list of protective devices above then you can see that their capacities are:

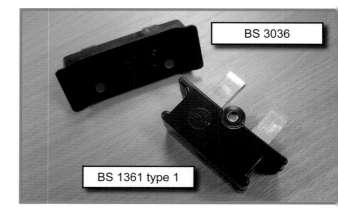

- BS 3036. A rewireable fuse of the type pictured is commonly found.
  It is the top one in the table (S1A).
  This can safely "break" a fault current of 1kA or 1,000A.

- BS 1361 type I. The cartridge type pic tured is a BS 1361 type I. It is the fourth one down the table and can break up to 16.5kA or 16,500A.

- BS 1361 type II. This is the one immediately underneath the BS 1361 type I fuse on **p50 OSG**. This type is the one usually found at the mains position, which the local power company use as a main fuse or "cut out." It can break up to 33kA. These are pictured on **p21 and 22**.

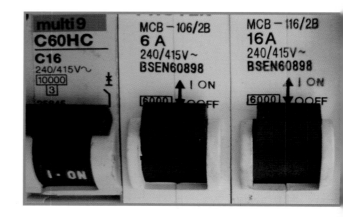

The mcbs are listed at the bottom of the OSG table. To know how many amps these will clear during a fault you simply look at the breaker. In the picture here the left hand mcb is rated at 10kA and the other two are rated at 6kA. The relevant number is within a rectangle on the front of the mcb. There are also older BS 3871 mcbs. These have an "M" number marked on them. An M6 breaker will break up to 6,000A and so on.

On **P50 OSG** you will see a listing for BS88 type fuses. These are industrial types and you should never see them on your domestic adventures.

Before we leave protective devices, there is one more thing to cover. Please look now at **p51 OSG**. Here you should see table 7.2B. This table explains the difference between B, C & D type mcbs. Ignore types 1, 2, 3 & 4. These are the older version of the modern B, C and D type mcbs and you cannot buy them anymore.

Looking now at these mcbs, the table tells you how many times the rated current you need to trip them instantly. I will take the worst-case scenario. The multiples are:

- B type   5 times
- C type   10 times
- D type   20 times

In other words, then, taking say a 32A mcb you would need a current to trip each type of:

- B type   160A   (5x32)
- C type   320A   (10x32)
- D type   640A   (20x32)

So, you may say "so what." Well my point is this. Turn to **p92 OSG** and check out the maximum earth loop impedance figures for 32 A mcbs. For each now you will see maximum figures of:

- B32   1.20Ω
- C32   0.60Ω
- D32   0.30Ω

As you are now familiar with Ohms law you may spot it working here. As you look down the two lists above, you can see that you need twice the current to trip a D type compared to a C type, therefore the loop for the D type must be half of the C type. This is then repeated in the relationship between the C type and B type.

This halving of maximum earth loop impedance figures can cause problems on your install. As an example of what I mean, our project bungalow's upstairs ring recorded an earth loop impedance of 0.51Ω. Therefore, only a B32 or C32, shown above, would comply with the 0.4 disconnection time for a socket outlet circuit. When you start testing for a living you will soon realise that 0.51Ω is a reasonable, average figure. My point therefore is to be careful when the wholesaler says he only has D type breakers in stock as you may be in for difficulties at paperwork time! The reason for the need of these different types is explained in the table on **P51 OSG**
In a domestic setting, you will usually get by with B type units apart from the following, which has happened to me on my travels!
Sometimes when fitting a number of SELV down lights in a kitchen on a single switch the mcb can trip when you turn on the fittings. There is nothing wrong with the circuit, it is simply a surge of current that can occur with transformers when they are first energised. The B6 mcb will trip if the surge is greater than 6X5= 30A. The quick fix is to swap the offending breaker for a C6. This requires a surge of 6X10= 60A and should cure the nuisance tripping. However, **p92 OSG** tells us the maximum earth loop impedance has now gone down from 6.40Ω to 3.20Ω. Obviously if my recorded earth loop impedance for the circuit is less than 3.20Ω, then I will be on my way home, all done!

Disconnection times

In BS 7671 there are many maximum disconnection times listed. In the event of an earth fault a fuse or breaker must quickly disconnect a faulty circuit. On a domestic install you need only know two.

- All fixed equipment must be 5 seconds maximum
- Socket outlet circuits 0.4 seconds maximum.

The reason for the difference is that regarding socket outlets you could be holding a faulty piece of equipment in your hand so it could do with disconnecting very quickly! You could argue that if you were caressing an immersion heater cylinder, at the time of a fault, you could also do with 0.4-second disconnection. That is a fair comment but that behaviour is outside the scope of this book!
From your previous readings, it can be seen that maximum disconnection times are linked to maximum earth loop impedance. To summarise:

- The lower the earth loop impedance.
- The more current flows during a fault.
- The faster the protective device disconnects the circuit.

In relation to mcbs and fuses, go now to **p89 OSG**. Here you will find listed maximum earth loop impedance figures for both disconnection times. It is a good idea to highlight the 0.4 and 5 second bit in the title of each table. The pages that concern you are:

- **P89 OSG**. BS 3036 rewireable fuses. 0.4 sec or 5 second tables.
- **P91 OSG**. BS 1361 cartridge fuses. 0.4 or 5 second tables.
- **P92 OSG**. All mcbs. 0.4 and 5 second table.

The only thing for you to note here is that there is only one table for mcbs. It means that in reality there is no such thing as different disconnection times for an mcb. As long as the earth loop impedance recorded is less than the maximum stated, then the device will trip instantly.

I am sure, if you have read this up to now you are eager to actually put a circuit in! Well now, you do not have much longer to wait. The job we are looking at is a new build dormer bungalow. We are going to run through this process slowly, one step at a time. This will cover any EIC you do up to full rewires. If you do one circuit at a house, you issue an EIC for that one circuit and not for the rest! Before we install there is just one more thing to mention again.

On an EIC you sign for three parts of the work:

- *Design.*
- *Construction.*
- *Inspection and test.*

We shall cover the first one in this section. It takes a designer to design an electrical installation so how can a bathroom fitter do it? The answer lies in the OSG. Here they have done all the maths for you to let you know what you can get away with safely. We shall now look at this book.
Go to **p4 OSG**. This is the contents section. Here you shall find section seven, entitled "final circuits". Now go to **p40 OSG**, we will start here first.

In this section the IEE have used "ball park figures" and assumptions for their circuit designs. The criteria and conditions are listed half way down p40. The first one is the main one so we will look at that. To calculate figures they have assumed that the "external earth loop impedance" (Ze) you have will be lower than their quoted maximums. These maximums are:

- TN-S 0.8Ω
- TN-C-S 0.35Ω
- TT 200Ω

This now introduces a new term Ze, or "external" earth loop impedance.

If you go back to **p12-13** you will see we previously did a loop impedance example on an imaginary cooker circuit. If you then go to **p19** you will see that I stated that a "system" is from the "sub-station to the playstation". To gel this together, you need to know that an alternative name for "earth loop impedance" is Zs or "system impedance:. In other words the measurement is taken from the end of a circuit.

This new term Ze or "external earth loop impedance" is a measurement taken at the consumer unit measuring back down the street supply only.

Ze testing is covered in detail in this book's inspection and testing section.

All you need to know here is that as long as your measured Ze is lower than the quoted maximums, you are ready to design. Now turn over to **p42 OSG** and let us look at how it is laid out. On this table, you will spot ring circuits and radial circuits.
Let us do an example together now to figure out how all this works, and do not worry, it is not as bad as it first looks!

Let us say you are to wire a lighting circuit. To find a solution we need to agree some facts and figures. Therefore, I shall assume

- The house is supplied via a TN-S supply.
- You would like to wire the circuit in 1.0mm² twin and earth cable.
- On this circuit are ten 50W down lights and six pendants.
- You pace out what you need and reckon on 45m of cable.

We are now going to design this circuit so it complies with BS 7671. The first job in hand is to work out the load on the circuit. We have:

- 10 X 50W down lights. This is then taken as 500W
- 6 X plain pendants. (We will assume 100W per pendant). This works out at 600W

- Therefore, the total load is 1100W or 1.1kW

Now we have to work out how many amps that will draw from the supply. From previous reading on **p14** you now know that current = watts/volts so:

- Current demand= 1100/240= 4.58A

Your next task is to select a device to protect the circuit. The logical rule here is that the protective device has to be equal to or greater than the current demand. Therefore, this circuit will work perfectly well with 5 or 6A protection. In other words, the breaker will never trip due to normal loading. We shall choose a B type mcb of 6A rating.

You now need to look at the tables. Turn the book round sideways!

1   Look down the first column until you find the correct protective device rating. You should now be looking at two rows ("bottom" of p42 and "top" of p43).

2   Next look at second column now and select your cable. This should now eliminate the second row as you are using 1.0mm² cable and not 1.5mm² cable.

3   Now on the selected row you can see three sub-rows, you need the middle one which covers a B type mcb.

4   Now go to the top right of the page to find the correct columns for your system. You should be looking at "TN-S" columns which are third and fourth from the right.

5   Now you need to decide which column you are to select. Our job is lighting so 5-second disconnection is to be selected. You should have narrowed this down now to the second of these two columns.

6   If you now link your column and row selected you should be looking at a maximum circuit length of 38m.

I-ON

Oh dear, this circuit will not work as we have a maximum length of 38m and need 45m to do the job in hand. You now need to re-evaluate the situation. Your only option is to make the cable bigger, so you will repeat the exercise now with all parameters the same except using the bigger cable.

7   Look down the first column until you find the correct protective device rating. You should now, once again, be looking at two rows ("bottom" of p42 and "top" of p43).

8   Next look at column two, and select your cable. You have abandoned 1.0mm^2 so should be looking at the second row at the top of p43. This is the 1.5mm^2 row.

9   Now you can see three sub-rows, you need the middle one again, which covers a B type mcb.

10 Now go to the top right of the page to find the correct columns for your system. You should be looking at the "TN-S" columns. These are, as before, the third and fourth columns from the right.

11 Now you need to decide which column you are to select. Our job is lighting so 5-second disconnection is to be selected. As before, you should have narrowed this down now to the second of these two columns.

12 If you now link your column and row selected you should be looking at a maximum circuit length of 59m.

    Now you are in business! You need 45m of cabling and you can fit 59m.

Congratulations, you have now become an electrical designer!

Before moving on, we will do another example.
A customer phones you and she requires the fitting of a new circuit for her 3.8kW built in oven. The supply is a TN-C-S and so being a fixed appliance will be on 5second disconnection times. There is an existing board with rewireable fuses fitted (BS 3036) and a couple of spare ways. Therefore, to save money and make the job simple we will run this circuit on a rewireable fuse. The run will be around 9m.

•   First we need to work out the load or design current .
    We know that current demand=P/V so I=3800/240=15.8A.

•   Now we need a fuse. Looking at our tables you can see that they do not make a 16A BS 3036 fuse. They do make 15A fuses, but this is too small so it has to be a 20A. For the purpose of this exercise I am not applying any diversity to this cooker. If you are not sure of the term diversity, please have a quick look at the end of this section.

Now it is off to the tables again. Turn the book sideways on **p44 OSG**.

1   First, we must find our protective device. Once again, there are two rows worth for 20A.

2   Next we select a cable, we will try 2.5mm² so can eliminate the second row as this is for 4.0mm² cable.

3   Now you should see five sub-rows. We need the second for a BS 3036 fuse.

4   Next, go to the right hand end columns to find the two columns for TN-C-S systems. You should be looking at the last two columns.

5   Again, we will pick five second disconnection as the job is supplying fixed equipment. You should now be looking at the very last column.

6   Now join up your selected row and column.

We have trouble! Our table states N3. If you turn to p 47 this will tell you that what you are attempting to do is not permissible because of cable overload.

Now we will have to re-design for compliance. Looking at the tables try it for yourself. The obvious alternatives are to use 4.0mm2 cable on our 20A rewireable fuse. This allows a maximum circuit length of 43m. Perhaps a cheaper way to do the task would be to change the protective device from a BS 3036 to a type B mcb. Simply doing this would give us a maximum cable length of 27m using our original 2.5mm² cable. As they say, "You pays your money and takes your choice!" Seriously though, sometimes a little thought can gain you compliance and save you time or money!

Please take a little time to digest these tables and the associated notes, as they are the cornerstone of your design procedure. Also take notice of fourth and fifth columns on the tables. These can put a restriction on where you install your circuit. By the way the majority of your work will be reference method 1. This method is clipped directly on a wall or plastered into the wall. Also take note that if your work is to be on T-T installations then you can use TN-C-S 5 second figures for your calculation on 0.4 and 5 second circuits. This is because these installations must be protected by an rcd. These are covered in part 7 of this book.

One other thing to discuss now is a table in appendix 8 on **p151 OSG**. This part used to be in BS 7671 but as the book has grown it has been put here! This part covers standard ring and radial circuits. In this table it explains your options for wiring socket circuits. You will note that the limiting factor is floor area, not socket numbers. It can be seen, therefore, that you could put 1000 sockets in a kitchen as long as you do not exceed the floor area. The reasoning for this is simple. The biggest load you would plug in would be a heater and how many could you plug in within an area before you would pass out from the heat?

Spurs are covered on **p153 OSG**. I won't repeat what is written only to explain that:

  • A "spur" is a radial circuit, which is connected into a ring.
  • A "non-fused" spur is a socket on the end of a spur wire.
  • A "fused" spur is a fused connection unit (spur unit) on the end of a spur wire!

While we are here, it is now time to bust a few myths I have heard over the years.

MYTH   *Wiring spurs is bad workmanship or "rough".*

spurs are so bad why do the institute mention them? It all depends what load you put on the end of , and how loaded the circuit is in the first place. Most of the time, it is no problem at all.

MYTH   *You can only spur from a socket outlet.*

he regulations do not state where you cannot spur from, therefore, you can spur from wherever you ke! That means you can spur from

- A socket
- A joint box connected into a ring circuit
- The ring connections in a consumer unit

MYTH   *It's all right to "spur" off a spur.*

his is incorrect. A spur may only supply a single socket, a dual or multiple socket or a fused connection nit.

MYTH   *If the consumer unit is full, you must not double up two circuits to create a spare way.*

his myth is also not strictly true. Hopefully when you design your new circuit, you will be confronted vith a nice consumer unit with plenty of spare capacity. Alas, this is not always the case so then you ave to look closely at the existing circuits. If the loading of two circuits does not exceed a fuse or reaker rating, then you can happily double them up to create that needed way. Maximum demand nd diversity is dealt with in the next paragraph, but for now a couple of obvious examples.

- A bell transformer on it's own circuit. This is very easily moved to say a lighting circuit.

- A small lighting circuit. If an existing circuit supplies say a few lights in a loft conversion or likewise, it could be doubled up with another small lighting circuit.

eedless to say, abuse of this doubling up would be blatant by:

- Connecting a shower and cooker to a common breaker or fuse in a consumer unit
- Doubling up ring circuits
- Doubling up an immersion heater with a ring circuit. This is specifically mentioned as a "no-no" at the bottom of **p154 OSG**

The only thing left to discuss now is diversity. If you look at all the breakers and fuses in your house and add them up, they would most likely exceed the 100A main fuse! A designer is allowed to apply diversity to circuits. In other words he is permitted to design in the fact that not everything is on all at the same time. Go now to **p6 OSG**. Appendix 1 is where this is looked at.

On **p85 OSG** are the ballpark figures for the assumed current draw of items of equipment. The two old favourites to give you an idea are a light fitting, which is taken as 100W a point and a cooker.

The cooker is a good example of maximum demand adjustment. If you look at the rating plate on a freestanding cooker it is usually around 12kW. Now doing our rough amperage draw maths, (4A per 1 kW) we would have a demand of 48 A. that should mean a 50A protective device and a monster cable to boot!

Looking at our table now a cooker is given as the first 10A + 30% of the remainder + 5A if the cooker control unit has a socket outlet fitted.

This would give us then:

1	The first 10A	10.0A
2	30% of 48A-10A= 38A of which 30% is	11.4A
3	Plus 5A if socket fitted	5.0A
	Total current draw	26.4A

Therefore now you can wire it in 6mm² with a 30/32A protective device like you have always done, but it is with the backing of the Institute of Electrical Engineers!

Turning over the page in your OSG now you can see the diversity tables. Your jobs are on the first column under type of premises. It is all very subjective; these are only guides for the designer. In most houses you can add a load without a second thought. Of course if a customer phoned up and wanted three 10 kW showers fitting that would be a different story!

The biggest load in a house is usually the kitchen so kitchen fitters take note:
You should usually fit a dedicated ring for your new kitchen.

After all the reading that you have done, you should be glad now to get your tools out! Here I shall advise on the construction side of things. Remember that to comply with Part P you will fill out and sign an EIC. On the document you have to sign for construction, in other words you are stating,

"I have put it all in properly!"

The pictures you shall see in this section were taken as I installed at our project bungalow. Before we start let us have a quick look at **p52 & 53 OSG.**
The first diagram shows floor joists with the method of wiring through them. To comply you have to either drill at least 50mm from the top or bottom or run the cable in notches. In notches, they show the cable in earthed steel conduit. This would turn a little job into a big one! It would suffice to use either proper joist plates as sold at the wholesalers or use steel conduit box lids. The lids are cheaper! Also look at the notes under the drawing, which show other requirements regarding maximum notch depth, maximum hole sizes and so on.

The second diagram shows a room with chevroned "zones". To comply with the regulations a cable, if less than 50mm deep has to be within the chevroned areas. If it is not in one of these "safe zones" the cable has to be covered in earthed steel. Oh and before you think it, metal capping is not good enough! It is such a big job to run cable outside the "safe zones", the rule of thumb is easy, **DO NOT DO IT!** Remember though on the flip side to all this, if your cable is greater that 50mm deep you can run it anywhere you like! Now we have the diagrams out of the way let me show you our job.

This is the back of a bedroom wall. Note here how I have used these zoning regulations to my advantage. Referring again to your OSG these "safe zones" run vertically and horizontally from all accessories. Therefore I have wired this light and socket point down through the same hole in the studding. I have then gone sideways to the switch.

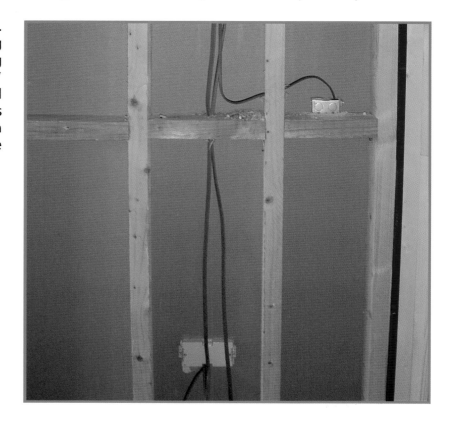

On this particular job I had a lot of trouble with the build. There were girders everywhere! Obviously you cannot drill them so circumnavigation is the only option! The thing I wish to show you here is that even though it is not the best job in the world, I have had to clip the cables along the top of the wall. Again this does comply, as there is a "safe zone" of 150mm around the top edge of the room. Note also the drilled joists.

Here is another example of clever zone installation. I have run the light feed and socket feed vertically down to the switch and swung sideways into the two-gang socket box. I have then carried on down the wall.

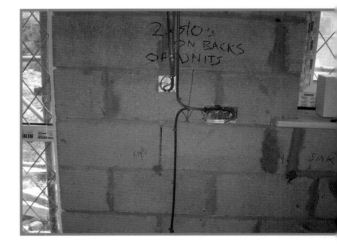

I hope these pictures clarify the way to wire a domestic installation. They also help to dispel anothe myth that has been around for all the time I have been installing.

MYTH   *Running cables horizontally is bad practice.*

Not so. The OSG clearly illustrates that this is compliant installation work.

MYTH   *Twin and earth cabling must be covered with "capping" or "channelling".*

This is also incorrect. Capping was once commonly used when cables were insulated with natural rubbe and plaster had a large content of very alkaline lime. Today's pvc cable is more chemically robust anc plaster is more neutral (less alkaline) in its ph make up. This bungalow was "dot and dabbed" In othe words the plasterboard was glued on the wall, so capping was not necessary.

The only place you need capping is where the job is to be plastered by hand.
The capping only provides protection from the plasterer's float.
On a rewire of an old property you would chase out the plaster to wire and again capping would not be required. Obviously the cable would be effectively in a trench and not subject to damage.
As you can see the construction part of your work is really quite straightforward. While I am on this section I shall cover a few tips I have picked up over the years to make your life simple and snag free!

Let us start with a nice easy one! When fitting boxes to breeze-block walls the fixings tends to be poor. If you drill in to the wall at an angle the screws will tend to secure the box much better.

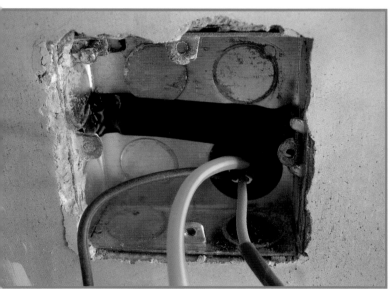

To cut down on nicked wires causing insulation faults this is a very handy tip. When you make off an accessory onto a metal box, make sure you tape across the screw head and any unused fixing holes in the back of the box. It only takes a second. Insulation faults are bad news and are to be avoided! Note the grommet fitted to the box entry. I cannot believe the amount of old jobs I go to where the electrician could not afford them!

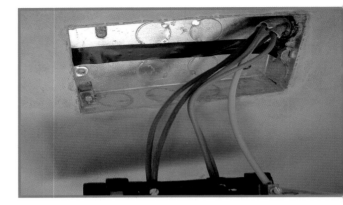

Again, here you see the back of this box taped. Also this shot shows that you should leave plenty of length on the conductors. It causes real problems when a customer wants a new socket fitting and the existing wiring does not reach! The wiring here *will* fold neatly back in there.

The previous picture also dispells another myth that is banded around the world of domestic installation.

MYTH *It is bad practice not to connect an earth wire to a flush socket outlet box.*

This is incorrect. The regulations say all "exposed conductive parts" shall be earthed. The socket box is sunk into the wall so is not "exposed". The box is earthed via the two socket fixing screws. This is only allowed if at least one of the fixing lugs is fixed and not sliding. Now some say to all this, " Ah, but the box becomes *unearthed* when you remove the socket!" My reply is that they should not be unscrewing the socket with the power on!

When you are terminating a light switch, do not forget to sleeve them "blues" as "browns" at the switches. As you know blue is the colour of a neutral conductor. At a switch the blue is usually a switched live conductor. You have to tick a box on your EIC titled "identification of conductors" and this is a prime failure example! Tape will suffice for this job if you do not posses brown sleeving. Please refer to the picture on **p41**.

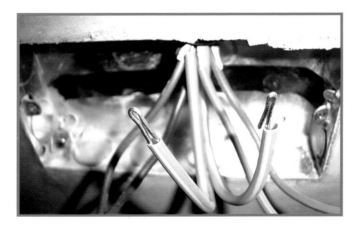

It is also good practice to "double over" conductors if two will fit in a terminal. At sockets I double over my cpc conductors. Not many do this but I think it is good practice as the earth wire is the most important and yet smallest wire! If you "double" the two 1.5mm^2 cpcs and pop them into the same terminal, that makes 6.00mm^2 worth!

While we are looking at general wiring in houses, it is time for a few more myths.

MYTH   *Joint boxes are bad practice or even banned!*

This is a strange one that I have heard many times. You can buy joint boxes over any counter. The regulations say all joints must be accessible for inspection and testing so it is bad practice to put them under laminated flooring or even worse, plastered into a wall! Joint boxes are an essential part of domestic work and are perfectly acceptable if fitted properly.

Here is one I did earlier! This is a joint box for a selv down light. This is done correctly with the sheathing cut back INSIDE the box, and all brown and green/yellow sleeving fitted. This is a "small" 20A joint box especially for the purpose, as it has to squeeze through a 64mm hole for the down light. Do not use connectors. That is bad and non-compliant work. Remember it will be so simple for your inspector to check if you are joining a scheme. If he sees connectors then you will not be joining! This is one of the few jobs that I do not enjoy doing as an electrician!

MYTH   *Open connectors are fine on the 12V side of a selv lighting transformer.*

Another non-starter I'm afraid. All electrical connections must be enclosed, irrespective of the voltage involved.

This is one of the new "choc-bloc" type enclosures which I have used for the 12V side of my down lights. The enclosure simply snaps shut over the connectors and then you install a securing screw.

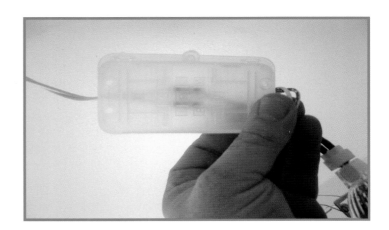

MYTH   *It is fine to just connect up the wires in a "hole" at the back of a wall fitting.*

The project bungalow was fitted with wall lights. It is common to see wall fittings installed without a box behind the fitting. This is forbidden by the regulations as it is stated that connections must go inside an enclosure. Some people fit architrave switch boxes available from all wholesalers.
I personally use pvc conduit boxes like this because it is bigger and most wall fittings will fit straight onto the mounting holes in the box.

MYTH   *It is bad practice to not fit smoke hoods on lights that are cut into a ceiling.*

This is quite a new myth as "smoke hoods" or "witches hats" are a recent arrival on the market. The truth of the matter is that your local building control interprets the rules the way he sees them. What you find is that some controls specify them and others do not. I have read a BSI (British Standards Institute) article recently. They have found that smoke hoods achieve nothing and cutting a hole in plaster board and replacing it with a metal/glass fitting does nothing to degrade its fire resistance. No fire hoods were fitted on the bungalow, as our "building control" did not specify them. On your jobs you must do likewise. Contact your local building control and ask their advice. As an alternative it is possible to purchase fully enclosed down lights that require no smoke hood.

Here I have fitted an earth clamp on the main water inlet pipe. As per **p24 OSG** and the regulations it is:

- On the consumers side of the stop tap
- As near as is practicable to the stop tap
- Preferably within 600mm of the tap!

I have a lugging tool to make off this cable but it would suffice to wrap the cable around the screw. In view of the fact each clamp comes with a free label, do not throw it, use it! The relevant tick box on your EIC is *"presence of danger notices and other warning notices."* If you do not fit the labels, you cannot tick this box and the installation cannot comply.

When you fit down lights on a ceiling it can be a struggle marking the ceiling without an extra pair of hands. Most of the time I am on my own. Therefore I have to improvise. Here I prepare to mark a set distance from a mark I have just made on the ceiling. I pull out the tape like this...

...And holding the tape measure in my left hand I can hold the distance required against the first mark. With my right hand I can scratch the ceiling with the hooked end of the tape.

Another secret you should know is the quick and easy practice of putting up a standard fluorescent fitting. It is not a good practice to hold a fitting against the ceiling with your head and hope it is straight as you put in the screws! You will invariably get it crooked on the ceiling. The easy way is to put the screws in pre-determined places and then place the fitting on the screws.

The back of a standard fluorescent fitting looks something like this. Take the measurements off the back of the fitting as shown and transfer them to the ceiling using the "scratching technique" shown above The fitting will then engage onto the "keyholes" and be perfectly straight first time.

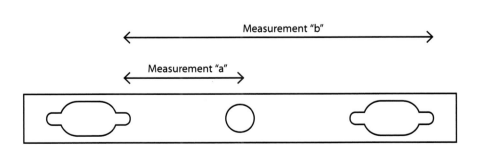

I have used the "scratching" tip and now have my screws in the garage ceiling. By the way, remember to leave the screws not fully screwed in at this stage or the fitting will not engage on them. When I get the fitting "engaged" I can simply tighten up the fixings. If you then want to, you can pop another fixing in to lock the fitting in position. I usually tend not to bother.

This is the start of my final fixing at the mains position in the garage. I have installed trunking to where the mains is going to sit. Also, I have knocked a hole through to the outside for the meter tails. The meter cabinet is on the reverse of this wall on the outside face of the garage. In accordance with **p28 OSG** I have used 25mm² pvc insulated and sheathed tails with a 16mm² earthing conductor. The little white wires you see are the telephone and door bell.

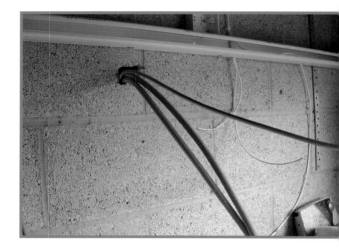

While we are on the subject of cables running through cavity walls, it is time to deal with another myth.

MYTH   *Electrical wiring in cavity walls is bad practice or "banned".*

This is incorrect. If it is banned, how am I allowed to run my tails through to the outdoor meter cupboard? Further to that, how can I ever wire any outside lights again? The answer is that cavity wiring is definitely on! The next argument put by the critics is that cavity wiring bridges the outer and inner leaves of the wall leading to "water transfer" from one wall to another. Well the wall is full of debris, "snots" of cement inside and cavity wall ties! Therefore, that is the end of that argument!
The only thing to be aware of is cavity insulation. If fitted after you have finished, then you can have a problem with cable de-rating. The reference method of installation would effectively change from M1 (Clipped directly) to M6 (Within an insulating wall). Look at **p40 OSG (item iii)** for a full explanation. In lay mans terms, this means that if a cable carries a maximum of say 30A clipped direct, then it can only carry say 25A in an insulating wall. The reason for this is simple. The insulation around the cable slows down the rate that the heat can escape from the cable when loaded.

I-ON

will run hotter and maybe too hot! The good news for you is that most cable design in **Section 7 OSG** listed as "M6" which means you can run it almost anywhere, including a filled cavity.

he final argument against cavity wiring is the lack of mechanical support for a cable. This is refuted on **101 OSG** where it advises us we can drop up to five metres without support. This conveniently covers 9% of houses. I have worked on many jobs where this has been done years previously and never seen damaged cable.

 you do have to run a cable in cavity, electricians have many methods to get the job done. I always carry few metres of "jack chain" in my tools. If you drop this down the void, you can hear it jangling when rying to "fish" it out. The ideal implement for fishing is an old metal coat hanger made into a hook. dditionally I form a "starting handle" out of it. When you insert it, you can spin it within the wall. The ther great advantage of chain over other methods is that if you are in the eaves of a loft space then you an throw a handful of chain at the top of the visible cavity. The sheer weight of it will drag it down the oid. In addition, because it is a chain it will go round obstructions within the void.

s you have seen previously, it is always preferable to avoid wiring hrough insulation. This picture shows a strange phenomenon hat is found sometimes on my travels. This is polystyrene sheet nsulation that has been in contact with pvc cabling. It looks ke the cable has burned into the sheet, but this is not the ase. Some sort of magical chemical reaction takes place. I am o scientist so this is my best description! The cable becomes tacky" and "sticky". The cables that did this had been installed, would guess twenty years or so, previously. If you come across a olystyrene cladded loft then the best policy is to clip away from his stuff.

Here I have now installed the consumer unit on the garage wall. The purpose of the trunking, as well as making cable entry easier is to comply with IP 4X requirements. This means that you cannot have a hole in the top of an enclosure that you can get a 1mm diameter wire through. I have complied here by running the trunking over the top of the consumer unit. The regulation applying to this is **713-07-01 BS7671**. If you are not sure what IP codes are all about, have a quick look at the special locations section **p59** where I have covered this in detail.

Before we move on, it is now time to deal with another myth.

MYTH   *Everything has to be "bonded", especially kitchen sinks.*

When the fifteenth edition of the regulations came out in 1981, the world went mad on "cross bonding", as it is nick-named. When the sixteenth edition arrived in 1992 these requirements were relaxed somewhat I cannot believe how much time I spent on my back stuck in a cupboard under a kitchen sink.
Well after all those years now I need not have bothered! This is stated half way down the page in **p26 OSG**
On the bungalow project there was a kitchen sink and a utility sink, but none were bonded.

This is an old sink I photographed on my travels This sink supplementary equipotential bond was correctly installed using 4mm² cable. This is the standard size of supplementary bonding cable for a domestic job as listed on **p162 OSG**

While we are on this subject then, a small treat for those of you that install central heating for a living. A lot of electricians and plumbers put a lovely row of earth clamps on all the pipes coming from the bottom of a boiler. **Do not do it!** All the pipes are connected on the plate on the bottom of the boiler and internally.
Bathroom locations can be a different matter with regard to bonding as they are classed as "special locations" This is looked at in the next section.

Little tips for you now while you are putting the installation in:

- When removing an architrave, the secret is to score down the sides of it, with a sharp knife, to break any paint seal. The next task is to run a junior hacksaw through the top mitre, there will be a nail or two in the joint. Then you should gently remove the architrave with a flooring chisel. When it is removed, do not hammer out the nails but pull them through with your snips and re-use them. This will ensure you do not "burst" the paint on the architrave.
- When you get floorboards up, remove the nails immediately; you know you will kneel on one!
- For getting from one place to another under floors, use a piece of trunking lid. In the trade this is called a "Charlie".
- When plastering, let the finish nearly set. Then float it off with a trowel and use a spray bottle, filled with water. Blend corners & joints with a wet paint brush.
- If the plaster has "gone off" and sets too fast, mix some salt into it.
  This will buy you some more setting time.

I-ON

- For wiring sockets, it is handy to get yourself a "bendy bar". This is a bar about 400mm long, about 13mm in diameter and bent in a vice. The bar requires a gentle radius on it. When you knock behind a skirting board to wire a socket, you won't force the skirting board off the wall.
- When wiring the sockets, try to get the cores in the same orientation as the socket itself. In other words, if the "L" terminal is to the right, as you look in behind it, wire the cables with the brown to the right. This way when connecting up the cores do not have to cross inside the box. This will cut down on insulation faults.
- When wiring main equipotential bonding conductors, if the gas and water are close together, wire one 10mm^2 green/yellow cable. At your first termination, wrap the cable around the screw. Do not cut the cable; it must stay unbroken.
- Write markings on a cable using a permanent marker, it won't rub off!
- When marking up for the fitting of a flush socket box put your fingers between the box and the skirting board and mark round it. When you fit the box, there should be this "finger gap" between the bottom of the box and top of the skirting board. When you finish the task the socket will sit flush on top of the skirting board, with no unsightly gap.
- If installing "back to back" socket boxes, remember to drill through the wall at an angle. If you chisel out on both sides of the wall, it may collapse.
- If you do have a wall chasing accident, do not despair. Cast the box in position with finish plaster, it will set like rock.
- Instead of measuring the height of every switchbox, cut some wood and use it as a staff.
- When you work in a loft full of fibreglass, try not to weep! Seriously, when you come out and clean up, do not use hot water. The water will open up the pores in your skin allowing the glass to penetrate and irritate further. Though uncomfortable, stone cold hand and arm washing is the order of the day.

While we are here now, a brand new myth for you.

MYTH   *Sockets and switches must go at Part M heights on all new work.*

This is not quite so. The requirement only applies to new build, not rewires. The law says if you rewire a house it must not be "any less hospitable" than it was before the work started. On the strength of this, if you are doing a house extension or full rewire, the heights of the new can be the same as the old. Stipulated accessory heights for new build are shown on **p155 OSG**.

And while we look at kitchens, I have come across a few other myths during my short teaching career.

MYTH   *It is incorrect or "rough" to wire sockets under sink units, to supply the built in appliances in the adjacent units.*

I am not sure where this one originates from. In general contracting, it is done all the time. The reason being, it is quick and easy. The argument about the faulty waste pouring water onto the under sink socket does not hold water (excuse the pun!) because you could have a leak upstairs and the same problem may occur anywhere else in the house. And while we are still on kitchens....

MYTH *You must fit spur units above the worktops to supply sockets behind the fridge or othe. appliances.*

There is nothing in the regulations regarding this. Therefore only do this if it is specified. Again, this is a regular myth that kitchen fitters bring to me when attending courses. Sounds like a lot of unnec-essary work to me!

MYTH *It is wrong or "rough" to put a socket next to a sink, in a kitchen.*

The regulations do not specifically mention socket distances and sinks anywhere in BS 7671 or the OSG. The NICEIC stipulate a minimum of 300mm distance for a socket from a sink. In a small kitchen I would not worry too much about it as most kettles have a 600mm lead, so you could still drop it in the sink!

The last thing to discuss in this part of the book is breaking meter seals and pulling "cut out" or main electricity company fuses.
Many years ago, when fitting a new consumer unit or doing a rewire, you had to fill out a completion certificate. This you handed into the local supplier. They then sent out an inspector who checked that the installation complied with the current regulations. If satisfied, the meter man would connect you work and re-seal. This was very inconvenient for some, so many electricians just said nothing, broke the seals and then connected up themselves! Worse still the suppliers have no records of what is sealed and un-sealed and many of their own staff do not bother sealing up anyway! If you do not believe this remember one thing, I was there!
Things have changed nowadays, the industry has deregulated and they have sacked most of the inspectors! So, as a domestic installer what do you do now to stay on the right side of the law? That i easy, put the onus on the supplier. They all have a common "official" policy of:

"It is a criminal offence to interfere with our equipment"

However, when you speak on the phone there are differing "unofficial" policies.
Differences encountered within the trade are:

- Some say break the seals, do the work, connect the job up and inform them at completion.

- Some say nothing at all as in "not interested!"

- Some say make an appointment to get the electric man round to break and remake your seals. He will not test your work though, it is not his job!

- Some say they will come round and fit an isolator after the electricity meter, to make your job easier. Some even come and fit it for free!

My advice for you is to talk to your local supplier and get them to fit an isolator, immediately after the electricity meter. As stated they will do this for free or for a nominal amount. You would be, as a Par P electrician, better off having the local electricity board as a friend rather than an enemy!

Part 6 of BS 7671 deals with "Special installations and locations." These are many and varied but the only one that usually concerns us is "rooms containing a bath or shower" Note that Part P also lists amongst others, kitchens as special locations. *This is only for notification purposes.* To comply with Part P you need to comply with BS 7671 so bathrooms are what we will concentrate on. To start off I shall state the bathroom myth.

MYTH   *To comply with the regulations you have to destroy a bathroom with earth wiring.*

This causes no end of problems for electricians and Part P domestic installers alike, but the task of compliance is usually over-rated. I have been to many jobs containing unnecessary ugly supplementary equipotential bonding conductors and visible earth clamps. A lot of this is not needed. The secret to doing this type of installation is to take a step back, have a think about it and proceed within the regulations AND to your advantage!

Now go now to **p30 and p31 OSG**. Here you find very good diagrams explaining the "zoning" that exists in rooms containing a bath or shower. What the regulations state is that:

'Local supplementary equipotential bonding ...shall connect together the terminal of the protective conductor of each circuit supplying class I and class II equipment in zones 1,2, and 3 and extraneous metalwork in those zones."

In layman's terms, this means that within these three-dimensional zones you must connect all circuit wiring, except selv, to the bathroom's pipework and exposed metalwork. This bonding can be achieved by a combination of:

- A supplementary bonding conductor (4mm^2 green and yellow cable)
- Reliable metal pipe work
- Circuit protective conductors within the twin and earth cable or flex

The basic reasoning for this work in a room containing a bath or shower is standard EEBADS technology. In the event of an earth fault on the installation all the metalwork in the bathroom will rise to the same voltage. Therefore, hopefully the pd (potential difference) or voltage across a victim will not be too shocking! The following pictures depict a real job to illustrate that it is not as big a job as you would first suppose. As we go through this project together, keep your OSG open to look at the diagrams!

This picture shows a bathroom through the door:

- The fan heater is in zone 2
- The ceiling light is in zone 2
- The shower is within zone 1

The cpcs of the circuits supplying these three items need connecting together. The pipe work in this installation is copper. It also needs connecting. Under the plastic bath is a built in Jacuzzi pump. The Jacuzzi and fan heater are supplied on the upstairs ring circuit.

Turning to the right now you can see the sink. Above this is a vanity light. This is also connected to the lighting circuit. It is in zone 3 The pipework to this sink is copper.

have turned right again now and am almost facing the entrance door. You can just see the edge of it in the right of this picture. Here is an electrical towel rail which is also just inside zone 3. The towel rail is also supplied via the upstairs ring circuit.

The picture here shows the outside of the bathroom. To the top is a two-gang switch. These switches are for the bathroom and landing lights. At the bottom of the wall are a two-gang socket and the spur unit. The spur unit controls the bathroom towel rail heater on the other side of the wall.

Before we start then let us summarise. This is at first glance a complicated job! To comply I have to connect together all electrical equipment and metalwork within the zones. This means I have to somehow connect together the following:

- Towel rail
- Vanity light
- Down-flow heater
- Ceiling light fitting
- Shower
- Jacuzzi
- Hot pipes
- Cold pipes

The secret to this job is that you do not have to "link" the ends of the circuits. Furthermore, we can use a cpc to bond, so before we start, we already have connected together:

- The down-flow fan,
  Jacuzzi and towel rail (same circuit)
- Vanity light and ceiling light
  (same circuit)

This has simplified the job somewhat as we now only need link the cpcs of the:

- Shower circuit
- Lighting circuit
- Ring circuit
- Pipework

We will now do this job one step at a time. By the way, the total time for this supposed "nightmare" project was around one and a half hours including stopping to pose for pictures!

If you are not up to speed with test instruments and method of use, you may want to look at the testing section before looking at this. If you are happy, then read on!

The very first job is to perform a safe isolation of all the circuits to be worked on. I have gone one stage further and switched off the whole house.

I started outside the bathroom and I am linking the socket to the light switch. This effectively connects the ring circuit cpc to the lighting circuit cpc

Here I am installing a 4mm² green and yellow earth cable. A fibreglass rod is used to get the cable from "hole to hole." The bit of wall damage is due to wooden battens running across the wall at the points seen.

Before the 4mm² has been connected in, I am doing a quick check to make sure all is well on the earthing of these two circuits. I am using my multi-tester on its "low-ohm" setting and testing between the switch plate and socket WITHOUT the 4mm² connected. I have taken a reading of 0.61Ω.

The next task here is to re-check between the switch plate and the socket with the 4mm² now connected. This will confirm that it is connected into the switch plate and socket earth terminal. A 0.00Ω (dead short) confirms that all is well. The last job is to re-fix the switch and socket.

This is a reading from the light switch to the met at the mains and back to the socket, proving that there is some sort of earth between them before I bridge "the two circuits with the supplementary equipotential bonding conductor. It is therefore a sort of "series continuity test" across the two cpcs. This is not in any book, but a quick check just to put ones mind at ease. If one of these circuits were somehow not earthed then it would be "masked" by the 4mm² we are about to connect.

I would not turn the power on at this stage as I could have introduced an insulation fault due to "squashing" some wiring into the back of this switch or socket. This would be incorrect and most embarrassing if it went "BANG!". We will therefore move onto the bath end to bond the pipe work and shower now.

To re-cap then, putting this cable in has connected together all the cpcs of the power and lighting circuits.

This bath panel pulls off without any tools required. If you look in the **OSG** diagrams now you will see that if the panel were to be left like this, then the space under the bath would be a zone 1 part of the bathroom. This is denoted by a small asterix next to the bath on your diagram. This causes extra problems. I shall explain why at the end of this section, but for now, I shall concentrate on getting the task in hand out of the way!

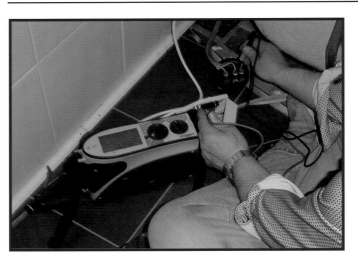

The bath panel has been removed now and I have found a switched spur unit under the bath for the Jacuzzi. In addition, there is a joint box fitted on the shower circuit. Within this joint box are old and new colour cables, so obviously the shower has been moved within the recent past. Just as before, on the landing, a quick check is required between the cpcs of the shower and ring circuit. This reading of 0.28Ω proves that there is an earth path from the ring cpc to the shower cpc via the met.

This picture shows the spur unit now connected to the shower joint box. I have also looped out of the joint box with another 4mm2 green and yellow cable to connect this part to the pipework. You can see this wire disappearing to the right of the picture. The only thing left to do now is re-fit the joint box lid.

To re-cap further, I have now connected the cpcs of the power to the shower to the lighting.

have fitted an earth clamp on the cold pipe in the background here. I cannot get to the hot pipe, so will deal with the hot to cold bond somewhere else. Before I connect, I am once again doing a quick check between the pipe and supplementary equipotential bonding conductor. A low reading of 0.09Ω again shows a good earth path from the pipe to the earth cable.

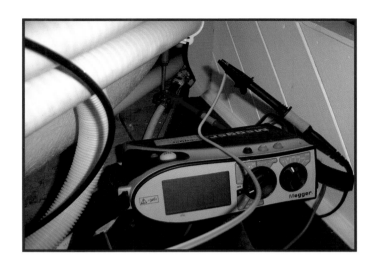

At the tap end of the bath, I have fitted a lug and earth label on the cable. If you do not have a crimping tool, do not worry. You may wrap the conductor around the screw of the earth clamp. However, do not forget the label. Remember, on your certificate, you tick a box stating: *"Presence of danger notices and other warning notices". You can't tick it if you've not fitted it!*

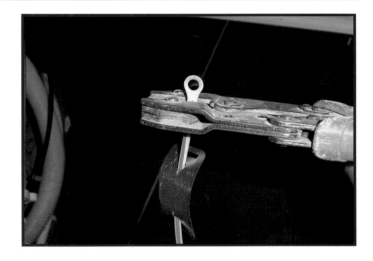

This is the finished job now. The bath panel is ready for refitting. The spur and joint box are not fixed. It is impossible to get a fixing into this restricted space so they are reinserted where they were originally. As the regulations say *"So far as is reasonably practicable!"*

To re-cap again, I have now connected the cpcs of the power to the shower to the lighting to the cold pipework.

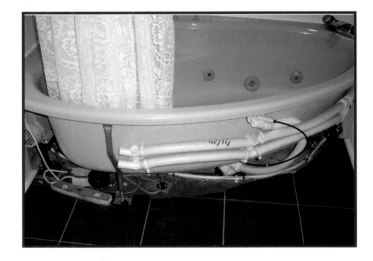

As stated previously I have only bonded between the circuits and the cold supply within the bathroom. I now need to link this bonding to the hot pipe, or so I thought. Under the sink, you can see the hot and cold leading to a monoblo tap unit. Effectively the pipes join here as they are soldered together so no further bonding i necessary.

To re-cap finally now, I have connected the cpc of the power to the shower to the lighting to the cold pipework to the hot pipework!

It can be seen that on this "difficult" installation I have used 3m of 4mm^2, one earth clamp and on 4/6mm^2 ring lug. More importantly perhaps there is nothing on show! Compliance is not difficult i one thinks about the job before proceeding. If you think I have been "jammy or fortunate" on this jol in some way, then have a look at your own bathroom and see how lucky you can be! This job did no have a "wet" heating system so I will now deal with a common misconception.

MYTH   *You have to fit an earth clamp on that lovely new "wet" towel rail or radiator.*

I think that after reading this section you can see that this is not strictly true. If the radiator has a "summer pack" heating element fitted, then the heater flex counts as the bonding. If not, then one only has to prove for good continuity between the radiator and the rest of the bathroom. If continuit is not good (say above 0.1Ω) then the clamp can go "within close proximity" of the bathroom. Thi means you could pop the clamp in the cylinder cupboard on the landing. You could, at a stretch, pu the clamp under the floor, as long as it remains accessible and you note it on the paperwork. Th regulations say that joints must be accessible for test and inspection.

Before I re-affix the bath panel, I now need to return to a comment that I made at the very top of **p56**. The other reason for the zoning regime is to make sure that the right equipment is fitted withir different parts of the bathroom, in relation to water penetration.
Turn to **p59 OSG** and all will be revealed.

Each zone has minimum requirements for water protection and is denoted by IP codes. (Index of Protection). Unfortunately, your OSG does not contain the key to these codes so they are reproduced for you below.

First Digit Number	Degree of Protection (Foreign Body)	Second Digit Number	Degree of Protection (Liquids)
0	No Protection	0	No Protection
1	Protection against ingress of large solid foreign bodies 50mm diameter	1	Protection against drops of condensed water
2	Protection against ingress of medium solid foreign bodies 12.5mm diameter	2	Protection against drops of liquid falling at any angle up to 15^0
3	Protection against ingress of medium solid foreign bodies 2.5mm diameter	3	Protection against drops of liquid falling at any angle up to 60^0
4	Protection against ingress of medium solid foreign bodies 1.0mm diameter	4	Protection against liquid splashed from any direction
5	Protection against ingress of dust in an amount sufficient to cause equipment malfunction	5	Protection against jets of water
6	Complete protection against the Ingress of dust immersion in water	6	Protection against strong jets of water or conditions found on ship's deck
		7	Protection against intermittent immersion
		8	Protection against indefinite immersion in water under a specific pressure

This is the coding to which all electrical equipment must conform. The first digit indicates the protection from solids and the second digit from liquids. Simply put, higher the number the more dust and watertight it is. If a code has an X in it, then it is not relevant to the standard. In the normal world of domestic electrickery, there are only usually four to look at:

- IP 2X   "finger protection" This is barriers and enclosures generally.

- IP XXB   This means the same as above, only the B stands for "finger barrier".

- IP 4X   This is a standard for the top of enclosures such as consumer units (so granny's knitting needles do not fall off a shelf and harpoon the top of her fuse board!). **See p47**.

- IP X4   "splashproof". This is the requirement for fittings in zone 1 and 2 of a bathroom.

Looking now at our bathroom again, **p30-31 OSG** tells us that the spur and joint box under the bath is in zone 1. **P59 OSG** then tells us that the accessories must be IPX4 (splashproof) and rcd protected. This would be very difficult and expensive to achieve. The most cost effective way to fix this is to look again at the diagrams on **p30-31 OSG**. Next to the bathtub pictures you will see a small asterix. The bottom of the page then tells us that the space under the bath is

- *"Zone 1 if the space is accessible without the use of a tool. Spaces under the bath, accessible only with the use of a tool, are outside the zones."*

So therefore, if we make this space accessible, only by use of a tool, then it automatically is removed from the zoning regime, and normal accessories can be installed.

Hey presto!

The space under our bath is now...
...NO LONGER A SPECIAL LOCATION!

The supplementary equipotential bonding project detailed here is nearly done now. In all the excitement, I have forgotten to put the power back on! What we will now perform is a quick insulation resistance check on our disturbed accessories and circuits.

Once again, if you are unsure of testing, have a read of the insulation resistance section of Part 7 (inspection and testing). Then return and read!

The quick and easy way to do this test is to:

- Turn OFF the WHOLE installation at the main switch.
- Turn ON all the breakers.
- If you now get an insulation tester, you can test at a convenient socket and test the whole house in one go. I have used the socket where I started on the landing. The theory is that as you test at a socket, you test **BACKWARDS** to the board and then **OUTWARDS** through all the breakers or fuses. (This method may not work on installations with certain types of electronic rcd or rcbos fitted).

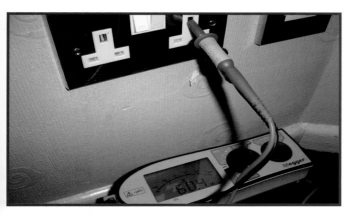

Do a test from live to earth and then from neutral to earth. Do not test between live and neutral as you risk damaging something within the installation with your 500V test voltage. The reading I got of 60 MΩ was a measurement of the whole installation including every appliance plugged in and is a very good reading.

- **P73 OSG** states that the minimum reading allowed is 0.5MΩ, with investigation required below 2MΩ.

- Usually if you do this sort of test on a house, you could expect to get readings down to 1MΩ or so but generally above 5MΩ.

- Only experience will tell you what is good or not so good. The one I got, above, is easily explained as excellent.

The very last job now is to turn on the power at the main switch and do quick earth loop impedance (Zs) reading, which I did at the landing socket. I got a reading of 0.42Ω.
A quick check in **p92 OSG** tells us that the maximum Zs for this circuit, which is a B32 mcb, is 1.20Ω so all is well.

Returning now to our project bungalow, there really is not much to write about! Looking again at **p30 & 31 OSG** our install is of the plastic pipe variety. The only electrical items within the zones were a fan (230V class II) and selv down lights. The lights and fan are on the same circuit so there is only one circuit in the vicinity. Therefore, there is nothing to bond to! This includes the chrome towel rail, as it was plastic piped. However there is one "special location" issue on our project. It was found that the height of the ceiling of the upstairs bathroom was 2.2m.

I-ON

Looking at your diagrams in the OSG you can see that the light above the shower tray is within zone1. The light to the left is in zone 2. Now looking at p69 OSG it can be seen that the fittings must be at least IPX4, which logically enough is "splashproof".

And these are the lights I ended up fitting. They are quite a good match for the rest of the lights fitted in the house. The lamp is up behind the splashproof glass you see here.

To finish now there is just a few more things to say again:

- Remember, if you are working on a metal piped installation, you do not necessarily need ugly clamps on show. If you can prove continuity of the pipe work from say a radiator to the cylinder cupboard, then, BOND IT IN THERE! Your customer will appreciate it much more!

- If a radiator or metal bath is plastic piped, do not bother bonding it!

- If the bath is metal and supplied on metal pipes then as long as you prove continuity between the bath and the pipes you need not bond it.
  This is because it is bonded via the pipework.

- If you think a little, you can nearly always hide bathroom equipotential bonding.

- If a bedroom has a shower tray in it then sockets must not be in zones 1, 2 and 3.
  Once outside zone 3, the sockets must be protected by a 30mA rcd.
  This is stated on **p59 OSG** note 1. This also counts on an en-suite bathroom without a door. It is effectively one room.

- If a bedroom has an en-suite, with a door on it then it is a proper bathroom and the "special location" ends at the doorway.

- If you come across other BS7671 "special locations" then read the book and take advice. I have been doing the job for a quarter of a century now and I have not come across them all yet!

will finish this section now with a couple more myths to be busted.

MYTH   *Electric showers must be supplied by a 30mA rcd unit, because it says so in the instructions.*

his is not mentioned in BS 7671 so you do not have to fit one! In reality   the shower manufacturers re "covering" themselves for incompetent, untested diy installation. You are not one of these people o these instructions do not apply to you! For those that are still not convinced by this, remember, you ave used EEBADS to design the circuit. It will disconnect within 5 seconds if a fault occurs and while his is happening all the metalwork in the bathroom will rise to the same voltage so if it does blow up vhile you are showering, you should be blissfully unaware apart from the shower stopping or running old!

MYTH   *You cannot put a light switch on a wall in a bathroom.*

es, this was once true, but not for such a long time! **p59 OSG** clearly allows "switchgear" within zone of a bathroom. It is still attacked by electricians and shows how long winded the process of change an be. Further more this page also shows that you could use a larger bathroom as a laundry room, as ou sometimes see on the continent. The only requirements are that the washer or whatever must be 0mA rcd protected and wired on a fused connection unit (spur unit).

Congratulations! If you have read and followed all the instructions up to here, you have now DESIGNED and CONSTRUCTED your installation to the standards laid down within BS7671. The last job now is to inspect your work, test it and finally leave the customer a certificate to say you have. The correct term for this process is "initial verification". To kick off now an old myth,

MYTH   *Initial verification and certification is very difficult or skilled work.*

This is just not so. Even though many people dread testing and paperwork, it is quite generic. In other words, once you do one, the next will be more or less the same.
This used to be not such a big deal on domestic work as BS 7671 is not the law, merely a code of practice. In today's world however, Part P *is* the law and to comply with the law you have to comply with BS 7671, and to comply with BS 7671 you have to certificate your work. So now, there is no escape! An EIC contains three parts:

- The certificate   **(p129-130 OSG)**

- A schedule of inspections **(p131 OSG)**

- A schedule of tests   **(p132 OSG)**

The certificate is pretty straightforward so we will come back to that later. For now, we will concentrate on the other two starting with the schedule of inspections.

Inspection

In this section, we will look at the inspection schedule and will fill it out. It must be said that there are a huge amount of certificates on the market. Each Part P scheme provider issues their own. All these certificates are always based on the model given in BS7671 so that is what I have used on the project. As you read this section, it is best to have your OSG open starting at section 9 on **p62 OSG**.

Your work must be:

- Inspected first and tested secondly, – not the other way around!

- *"Correctly selected and erected"* – have you put in the right equipment and installed it correctly?

- *"Not visibly damaged so as to impair safety"* – obviously!

- Fitted with equipment marked to CE, BS or equivalent standard.

The inspection checklist is in the form of a tick sheet. One of these is shown on **p131 OSG**. The main items on it are listed on **p62-65 OSG**. Remember this tick sheet covers all types of installations so do not be frightened by some of the terms in the boxes. Some of these boxes you will never see on a domestic job.

If you join a self-certification scheme, your scheme's inspection schedule will have most of these "odd ball" boxes removed. Therefore, it will be much simpler than this one.

As stated, on the bungalow project we are doing a BS 7671 style certificate. On an inspection schedule, you have two options to fill a box:

- **A tick:**
  inspection task is successful and recorded.

- **N/A:**
  inspection task is not applicable and not recorded.

You cannot put in an X indicating a "fail". It is a new job and is not allowed to fail! Fails are only relevant to periodic reporting on old jobs, which is outside your scope. On this schedule of inspection, I have also shaded the boxes that will never, ever concern you. In my time in contracting, I have never come across them on a domestic installation so do not dwell on them! If there are any unshaded boxes, which you do not understand, do not worry! I shall explain below.

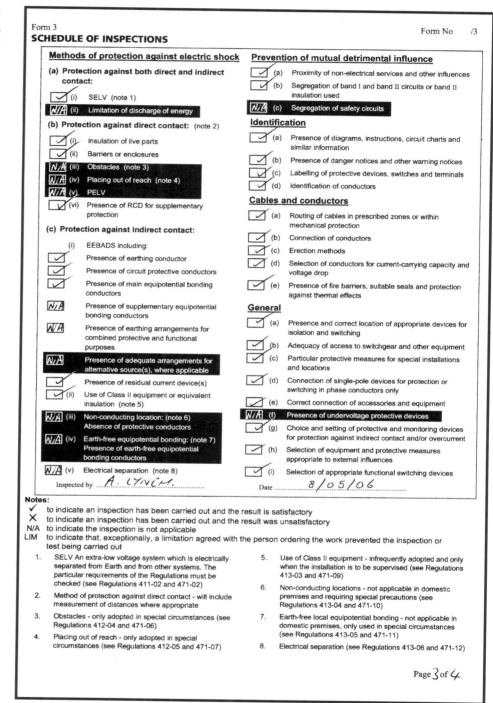

Form 3
SCHEDULE OF INSPECTIONS   Form No   /3

Methods of protection against electric shock

(a) Protection against both direct and indirect contact:
- ✓ (i) SELV (note 1)
- N/A (ii) Limitation of discharge of energy

(b) Protection against direct contact: (note 2)
- ✓ (i) Insulation of live parts
- ✓ (ii) Barriers or enclosures
- N/A (iii) Obstacles (note 3)
- N/A (iv) Placing out of reach (note 4)
- N/A (v) PELV
- ✓ (vi) Presence of RCD for supplementary protection

(c) Protection against indirect contact:
- (i) EEBADS including:
  - ✓ Presence of earthing conductor
  - ✓ Presence of circuit protective conductors
  - ✓ Presence of main equipotential bonding conductors
  - N/A Presence of supplementary equipotential bonding conductors
  - N/A Presence of earthing arrangements for combined protective and functional purposes
  - N/A Presence of adequate arrangements for alternative source(s), where applicable
  - ✓ Presence of residual current device(s)
- ✓ (ii) Use of Class II equipment or equivalent insulation (note 5)
- N/A (iii) Non-conducting location: (note 6) Absence of protective conductors
- N/A (iv) Earth-free equipotential bonding: (note 7) Presence of earth-free equipotential bonding conductors
- N/A (v) Electrical separation (note 8)

Inspected by *A. LYNCH.*   Date *8 / 05 / 06*

Prevention of mutual detrimental influence
- ✓ (a) Proximity of non-electrical services and other influences
- ✓ (b) Segregation of band I and band II circuits or band II insulation used
- N/A (c) Segregation of safety circuits

Identification
- ✓ (a) Presence of diagrams, instructions, circuit charts and similar information
- ✓ (b) Presence of danger notices and other warning notices
- ✓ (c) Labelling of protective devices, switches and terminals
- ✓ (d) Identification of conductors

Cables and conductors
- ✓ (a) Routing of cables in prescribed zones or within mechanical protection
- ✓ (b) Connection of conductors
- ✓ (c) Erection methods
- ✓ (d) Selection of conductors for current-carrying capacity and voltage drop
- ✓ (e) Presence of fire barriers, suitable seals and protection against thermal effects

General
- ✓ (a) Presence and correct location of appropriate devices for isolation and switching
- ✓ (b) Adequacy of access to switchgear and other equipment
- ✓ (c) Particular protective measures for special installations and locations
- ✓ (d) Connection of single-pole devices for protection or switching in phase conductors only
- ✓ (e) Correct connection of accessories and equipment
- N/A (f) Presence of undervoltage protective devices
- ✓ (g) Choice and setting of protective and monitoring devices for protection against indirect contact and/or overcurrent
- ✓ (h) Selection of equipment and protective measures appropriate to external influences
- ✓ (i) Selection of appropriate functional switching devices

Notes:
✓ to indicate an inspection has been carried out and the result is satisfactory
X to indicate an inspection has been carried out and the result was unsatisfactory
N/A to indicate the inspection is not applicable
LIM to indicate that, exceptionally, a limitation agreed with the person ordering the work prevented the inspection or test being carried out

1. SELV An extra-low voltage system which is electrically separated from Earth and from other systems. The particular requirements of the Regulations must be checked (see Regulations 411-02 and 471-02)
2. Method of protection against direct contact - will include measurement of distances where appropriate
3. Obstacles - only adopted in special circumstances (see Regulations 412-04 and 471-06)
4. Placing out of reach - only adopted in special circumstances (see Regulations 412-05 and 471-07)
5. Use of Class II equipment - infrequently adopted and only when the installation is to be supervised (see Regulations 413-03 and 471-09)
6. Non-conducting locations - not applicable in domestic premises and requiring special precautions (see Regulations 413-04 and 471-10)
7. Earth-free local equipotential bonding - not applicable in domestic premises, only used in special circumstances (see Regulations 413-05 and 471-11)
8. Electrical separation (see Regulations 413-06 and 471-12)

Page 3 of 4

I-ON

65

It is quite self-explanatory. However, a few tick boxes are worthy of a mention.

On the first column:

- *"Presence of supplementary equipotential bonding conductors"*
  This was marked N/A because as you have seen in the previous chapter, I have not done any bathroom bonding on the bungalow!

- *"Presence of earthing arrangements for combined protective and functional purposes"*
  The only instance you will see of this is if you buy an rcd with a little cream wire attached to it. It is a functional earth, in other words it needs an earth to function.
  My job did not have one so the box got an N/A.

- *"Use of Class II equipment"*
  I fitted three double insulated fans in the bathrooms and utility room.

- *"Electrical separation"* I did not fit any shaver sockets in bathrooms.

And on the second column:

- *"Proximity of non-electrical services and other influences"*
  No wiring lying against hot heating pipes I hope!

- *"Segregation of band I and band II...."* This box means that you have not put any bell, telephone or alarm wires in a trunking or enclosure with your mains wiring. Band I wiring is bell wires and alarms etc, and Band II wiring is normal 240V circuitry.

- *"Identification of conductors"* This one is for you to state that you have sleeved those blue wires as browns at light switches. In addition, in a consumer unit all wiring must be in the same "order". In other words if you wire a circuit to breaker number 2 then the neutral and cpc must go in the corresponding number 2 terminals.

- *"Selection of conductors for current carrying...."* You have used your OSG to design your circuit so you can automatically tick this box with the blessing of the IEE!

- *"Connection of single pole devices for protection...."* This is a *visual* inspection to say that all your switches and breakers are installed in the live conductor. You will test this electrical "polarity" later, so if you are unsure of this term at this stage, do not worry.

- *"Choice and setting of protective devices...."*
  Have you put the right rating of fuse or breaker in!

It can be seen that the majority of these are very common sense ticks. For instance, it would be foolish to go round re-checking the "connection of conductors" when you have already given all the connections a quick tug as you are fixing back the accessories. In other words:

- *You inspect the work as you put it in*

This is why it is frowned upon to test others work. It is quite impossible to sign off someone else's work "hand on heart" so to speak. Here, you have installed the work, you know it is correct so you can fill out this schedule. You can also do it at the end of the job sat at the customer's kitchen table while having a cup of tea!

One tick box that needs looking at before we move on is the one in the second column called:

- *"Presence of diagrams, instructions, circuit charts and similar information"*

This is a requirement of chapter 51 of the regulations and is one of the most neglected regulations of all. It is not sufficient to just mark the mcbs or fuses. You must leave a chart with more information. The regulation number that covers this is BS7671, 514-09-01. If you do not have your BS7671 to hand, do not worry, a compliant circuit chart is shown below.

WAY NO.	DESCRIPTION	POINTS SERVED	CABLE TYPE	CABLE SIZE LIVE	CPC	EEBADS	MCB TYPE	RATING A	IR TEST CAUTION	notes
1										
2										
3										
4										
5										
6										
7										
8										
9										
10										
11										
12										

This is a chart that I did myself on the pc and is quite satisfactory for the job. All the information on this chart you would get from your paperwork and your memory as you did the job! Your scheme inspector will expect to see one on every job. If you put in a single circuit then you are only obliged to fill in one line of this chart.

I-ON

Now you have seen the inspection schedule, it is time to deal with a few myths.

MYTH   *When you do a certificate for a single circuit at a house, you have to inspect and test the whole house or somehow become responsible for it.*

Not true. If you were to wire say a central heating system, then your inspection, test and certificate would only concern the work you do. You would, however, be obliged to comment on the existing installation.

MYTH   *When you install a single circuit, the sub-standard main equipotential bonding is not your problem.*

Not true. You have seen that the inspection schedule has tick boxes for all the earthing in the house. If the main bonding is inadequate or non-existent then you have to make it compliant.

MYTH   *If you do a consumer unit upgrade the existing wiring is not your concern.*

Definitely not true! You must be very careful when doing a consumer unit change as you DO inherit everything connected to it. This means you must inspect and rectify any defects found. Of course, there may be defects that you cannot see so my general advice is not to get involved with this work it is fraught with danger. It seems that some electricians change units without a thought, no matter how old the wiring. Also, a lot of electricians trigger a consumer unit change because of lack of capacity in the existing unit. My advice in this scenario is to fit a new, second consumer unit, if possible. You are then most definitely, not responsible, for any problems on the existing installation. Meter blocks are available to connect all the tails into, so there is no need to attempt to jam two sets of tails in anywhere! Please refer to **p50** on advice with regard to removal of the main fuse to do main work on an installation.

This completes the inspection part of initial verification and now we can move on to the testing part.

Testing

Before you test anything at all you will need testing equipment of some description. The market is awash with many types of all shapes, sizes and manufacturers. Some instruments are sold as single units, so you would need a number of these, while some instruments perform all the tests within a single unit.

All instruments are of a similar standard.

If you are not using the same unit as me you will have to read your tester's manual so you are on the same settings as me. It is most important that we are all "singing off the same hymn sheet", so to speak!

When testing, you will also require some sort of voltage indicator to check for a live supply. All instruments possess this facility as they have a voltage range. However, you may find it cumbersome for some jobs and will probably get yourself a purpose made test lamp. Again these come in all shapes and sizes. One more essential item is a "proving unit". This is a battery powered device that can light your voltage indicator. This will be handy if you work somewhere with no supply present.

Testing can involve working with voltage and so it goes without saying that caution is the order of the day. If you follow my instructions, you will not come to much, or cause much harm! The next thing that must be discussed is HSE GS 38.

This is a memorandum published by the Health and safety executive on test leads and probes.

To summarise, if you do not have it to hand, it says that leads should be:

- *Flexible; not too short; not too long; coloured; sheathed and fused.*

It also states that the test probes should be:

- 4mm maximum bare metal; preferably 2mm or fitted with sprung sleeves and have finger barriers.

All equipment that you buy from reputable sources will be GS38 compliant. Now on a word of caution it must be said that a probe with a tiny exposed tip may not make proper contact with a live part. This will lead you into thinking something is dead, when in fact it is still live! This is highly hazardous so generally I trim back the insulation on a tip to the full 4mm. Do not trim more than this or you will be in trouble with your inspector. Finally, if you value your life and/or self-cert scheme membership, get rid of the volt-stick and neon screwdriver! These items of "test equipment" are a big no-no with any inspector.

The testing procedures and order of testing are from **p62- 82 OSG**.

Before we start on the testing there are a few last points I need to make:

- You will note that my order of testing is different to the order depicted in OSG. I have deliberately altered the order to make the testing much simpler to perform.
- At the start of each test you will see the complete list, with the current test highlighted.
- As each test is performed I am going to fill the schedule of tests.

The project bungalow was a "new build". As such, it was built with no electrical supply present. Bef
the supplier arrived to energise the installation:

- I had "first" and "second" fixed the full installation including main equipotential bonding
  gas and water.

- I had also fitted the consumer unit.

- I had also connected the meter tails into my consumer unit. The other end of the meter ta
  were coiled up in the outside meter cupboard, ready for the supplier's representative.

- Testing was to commence as soon as the power was put on.

Incoming polarity test **P78 OSG**

Mains live test	Incoming polarity test
Mains live test	Prospective fault current test
Mains live test	Ext. earth loop impedance test (Ze) or eath electrode test (Ra)
Circuit dead test	Continuity of protective conductors or ring circuit test
Circuit dead test	Insulation resistance test
Circuit dead test	Circuit polarity test
Circuit connected live test	Earth loop impedance test (Zs)
Circuit connected live test	RCD trip time test

The purpose of this test:

- To prove the electricity company's incoming live and neutral supply are not reversed.

When you work on a live installation you are governed by *"The Electricity at Work Act 1989"* This says that you have a duty for the safety of yourself and others. It is not difficult to adhere to. One of the most important items is safe isolation. This means proving that the switch or breaker is really off when it indicates off. Many electricians do not do this job as a habit. They walk up to a board turn off a breaker or a main switch and start work. This is a big no-no! It is foolish to assume that you have isolated just because the switch or breaker says "off." The bonus for you is that when you do your safe isolation you can complete the first test (incoming polarity) at the same time.

When the electric man put on the supply, I performed my safe isolation procedure straight away. I had no one available to photograph this so am repeating it for you. This is why you will see wiring connected in these pictures. Note that the main switch is in the off position and I am firstly testing for voltage between the incoming live and neutral. This shows a voltage present but does not tell me which one of these terminals is "live". It could be either one!

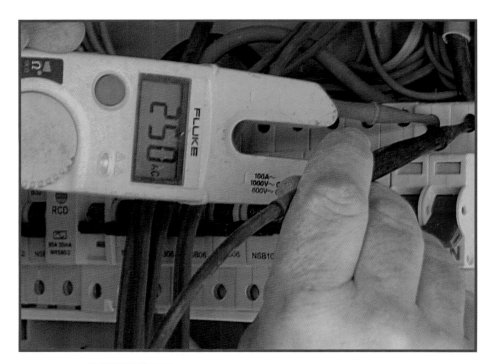

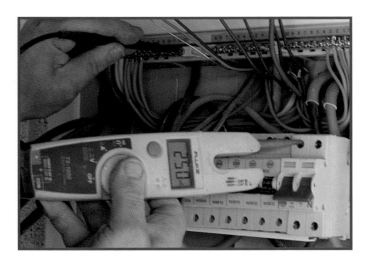

Now I am doing a test between live and earth. This is looking good now as the "live" incoming terminal appears to be really "live" on this incoming polarity check. Now there is just one more test.

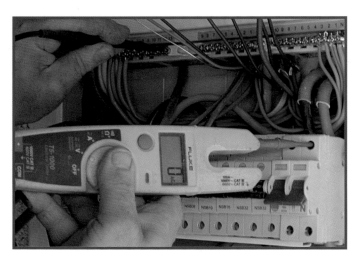

This is the final check on the incoming polarity. I am now testing between neutral and earth. There is no voltage present. This proves now that neutral and earth are at the same voltage and "common" to each other back at the sub-station. In addition, it proves that the live incomer terminal is in fact live! If the incoming supply was "back to front", you would get a voltage indication here.

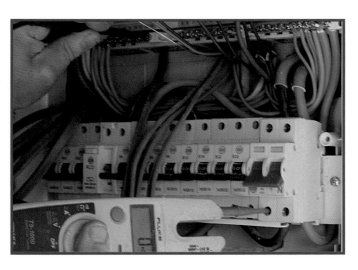

That completes the incoming polarity test, but now the next task is to check that the switch is really isolating the supply. Here, you can see me checking the live out going terminal of the "dead" side (bottom side) of the switch to earth and getting no reading, so all looks well.

Well I suppose your thinking now "Well that is that then." Actually, you would be very wrong. The final and *most important* part of this exercise is to check the operation of the voltage tester. It could have in theory, gone faulty, so in fact the outgoing side of the main switch could still be live!

A quick final check here, on the known live terminal, proves the voltage indicator is fine.

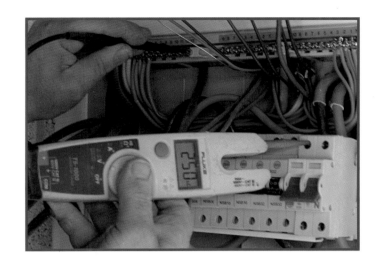

To summarise then, this very short operation has proved:

- The main switch really is "off"
- The incoming supply has definitely been connected properly with correct polarity

My final task now is to hang a sign on the wall adjacent to the board. You could padlock off the board now if desired. I was working with a limited workforce who are known to me so elected not to do so. In addition, nothing is connected in to the breakers and so turning on the main switch would not transmit a voltage anywhere on the job. Obviously, you will have to take each potential "lock off" on its own merits.

Prospective fault current test **P80 OSG**

Mains live test	Incoming polarity test
Mains live test	Prospective fault current test
Mains live test	Ext. earth loop impedance test (Ze) or eath electrode test (Ra)
Circuit dead test	Continuity of protective conductors or ring circuit test
Circuit dead test	Insulation resistance test
Circuit dead test	Circuit polarity test
Circuit connected live test	Earth loop impedance test (Zs)
Circuit connected live test	RCD trip time test

The purpose of this test:

- To prove that in the event of a fault, a fuse or breaker will safely disconnect the fault curren and not "blow up!"

If you need to re-cap on prospective fault currents, please go back and have a quick read of "Overcurren protective devices" on **p29**. When you are ready to proceed turn to **p50 OSG**.
At the top of the page is table 7.2A. Each device shown has a maximum current that it can safel disconnect in the event of a fault. The largest fault currents you will probably ever see in a domesti situation would be in the order of 2.5kA.

Most installations have a BS 1361 type II main cut out fuse and this is rated at 33kA. As you can see i really is a pointless test but as someone once said to me, "You can't pick and choose your regulations Therefore, we will do as we are told then! It is a quick and simple test. Two tests have to be done, a they would both cause a bang!

- Test between live and neutral (short circuit fault)
- Test between live and earth (earth fault)

I have now switched the tester over to its pfc (prospective fault current) setting and simply took a reading between live and neutral. The reading here of 1.41kA is committed to memory as we now have to repeat the test between live and earth.

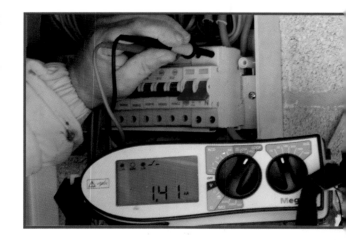

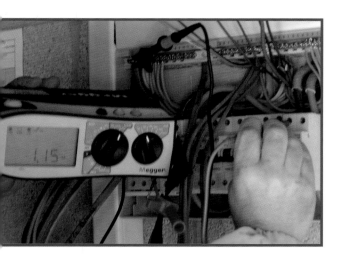

Leaving the tester on its pfc setting I now take a reading between live and earth. I will disregard this reading (1.15kA), as it is lower than the previous live to neutral reading. The highest reading is the worst case scenario and is the one that will be entered onto the schedule of tests.

The largest possible fault current on our project is 1.41kA (1,410A) and our main fuse can safely "break" 33kA (33,000A) in the event of a fault. Therefore, we can conclude that the installation is safe.

To summarise, this test has proved:

- If there is a large fault on the installation, then the main fuse can safely disconnect it without "blowing up" and perhaps cause a fire.

Mains live test	Incoming polarity test
Mains live test	Prospective fault current test
Mains live test	Ext. earth loop impedance test (Ze) or eath electrode test (Ra)
Circuit dead test	Continuity of protective conductors or ring circuit test
Circuit dead test	Insulation resistance test
Circuit dead test	Circuit polarity test
Circuit connected live test	Earth loop impedance test (Zs)
Circuit connected live test	RCD trip time test

The purpose of this test:

- Is to prove that there is a "true" electrical earth connection to the property you are working on.

The term Ze literally means "IMPEDANCE EXTERNAL" as in "earth via the street supply"
Over the years, on the job, this is a test, which I have seen performed wrongly, many times. It is in fac
a very simple test. The reason for the test is probably best illustrated by a job I went to a number o
years ago.

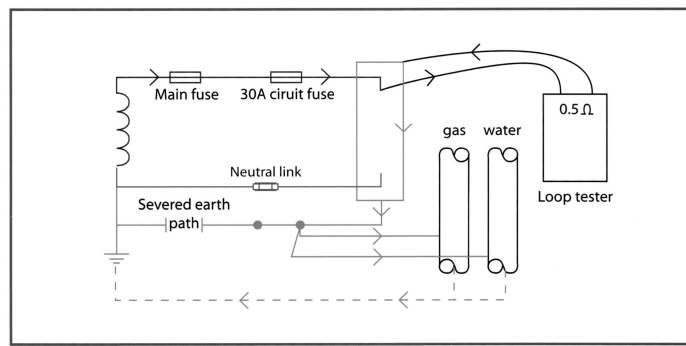

On this job with a TN-S supply, I performed a "minor works" . Minor works is covered later, but for now
you need to know that only the earth loop impedance (Zs) must be checked and recorded.

he diagram shows the sort of reading that I got at that time. This reading was fine, as the maximum 's for a 30A rewireable fuse on 0.4 second disconnection is 0.91Ω. This is illustrated on **p89 OSG**.)k then, so far so good. The arrows show the path of the test current.

he next year I was called back to rewire the property. When I removed the old wiring and bonding, his was an ideal time to conduct an external loop impedance test (Ze). What I found was that there vas NO EARTH on the house whatsoever! The reason why is illustrated in the diagram below.

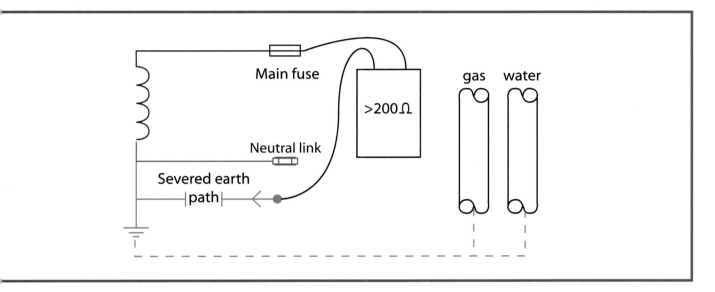

Vith the wiring and bonding removed. I performed the Ze test and found the return earth to the upply was severed in the street somewhere. The reason why I got an apparently good earth on the nitial visit was simple:

- The gas pipe into the property was steel
- The water incomer to the property was lead
- Therefore, the customer was getting a good earth through her neighbours property's main equipotential bonding conductors!

his problem is known as "parallel paths" and must be eliminated for the test. his is done by disconnecting the installation earthing conductor and measuring down this cable lone. It goes without saying then, that you must switch off! Remember, from previous reading, your rotection against indirect contact is EEBADS and you are about to remove it! o summarise then the sequence of the test is:

1 Switch off!
2 Perform safe isolation procedure
3 Remove the earthing conductor
4 Perform the Ze test
5 RECONNECT THE EARTHING CONDUCTOR!

The last step is so very important. Looking again at the diagrams you will see that leaving the earthing conductor out would not be detected on a property with good parallel paths. As I always reiterate to my students, at step five on the previous page:

You must not:

Answer the phone!

Answer the door!

Have your dinner or tea break!

Remember *you* are signing a pseudo legal document to say all is well. *You* were the last person to work on it and *you* left the earthing conductor out because *you* forgot. It does not bear thinking about Worse still, the job could have been 100 miles away and *you* do not want to be lying in bed drifting off to sleep thinking,

" Did I or didn't I?"

We will do the test now for real on our project.

Looking at our Ze checklist above, I already have the board switched off and checked for safe isolation. (I have done this in the previous tests)
I have disconnected the 16mm² earthing conductor from the main earthing terminal and put a lead and crocodile clip on it (top left of picture)
I have set the tester to its earth loop impedance setting and put my probe into the live terminal on the board.
Remembering step 5 now, I keep this figure in my head and immediately reconnect.

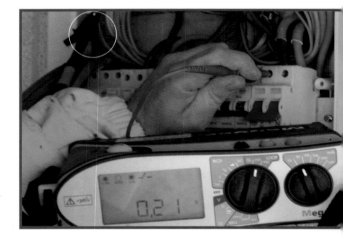

To summarise then, this test has proved that:

- This property has a proper electrical earth via the supply and not via any service pipework coming in to the property.

The test just described is applicable to TN-S and TN-C-S supplies. The test is almost identical on a T-T system. Now if you work on T-T installations then you are in luck! Many years ago, you needed a fancy and very expensive earth electrode resistance tester to measure a rod resistance value. Nowadays you can measure rods with a normal earth loop impedance tester as shown above. The reason for this is that a modern instrument can measure very high values of impedance. The test is done the same as above by disconnecting the earthing conductor from the met after safely isolating the supply. The figure is recorded in the relevant box on the EIC. If you go to **p129-130 OSG** you should spot where these figures should be inserted.

Now that we have a couple of test figures under our belt, it is a good time to start the schedule of test results, so this will be our next job. Everyone dislikes lots of paperwork so it is best to do it as you go. I always nail a schedule on the wall next to the consumer unit. As we do the circuit tests, I shall gradually fill out the schedule for you. The schedule of test results is displayed on **p132 OSG**.

Form 4

SCHEDULE OF TEST RESULTS

Form No   /4

Contractor: *M S P*

Test Date: *8/5/06*

Signature

Method of protection against indirect contact: *EEBADS*

Equipment vulnerable to testing: *DOWNLIGHTS + ALARM*

Address/Location of distribution board: *GARAGE*

* Type of Supply: TN-S/TN-C-S/TT
* Z_e at origin: *0.21* ohms
* PFC: *1.41* kA

Instruments
loop impedance:
continuity:
insulation:
RCD tester:

Description of Work: *NEW BUILD*

Circuit Description	Overcurrent Device * Short-circuit capacity: ...6..kA		Wiring Conductors		Test Results									
					Continuity			Insulation Resistance		Pol a r i t y	Earth Loop Imped-ance	Functional Testing		Remarks
	type	Rating I_n	live	cpc	$(R_1 + R_2)^*$	R_2^*	R i n g	Live/Live	Live/Earth		Z_s	RCD time	Other	
		A	mm²	mm²	Ω	Ω		MΩ	MΩ		Ω	ms		
1	2		3		*6	*7	*8	*9	*10	*11	*12	*13	*14	15

(column number labels: live=4, cpc=5)

I have made a start on the schedule and you can see that I have put in both the Ze and pfc readings now. The figures are at the top centre of this illustration. The mains end of the installation is now tested and finished. We have gone quite a way here now, setting the corner stone for the EIC. It would be fair to say that both these tests took a lot longer to write up than to actually do!

That is the first stage nearly done! Before moving on though, you must now put back on your designers hat. We have measured a Ze of 0.21Ω. We must now check this figure against our design criteria.

In part four of this book we saw that you can design with an "assumed maximum Ze". Therefore, the *measured* Ze figure must be lower than this maximum. To remind you then, this is a TN-C-S installation:

- This type has a design maximum Ze of 0.35Ω as per **p40 OSG**
- Our actual Ze reading was 0.21
- This means we are home and dry!

This now completes the first stage, the live testing of the mains. Before we start testing the circuits to be connected it is prudent to complete a little of the schedule of tests. It is fair to say that most people cringe when seeing all those boxes for the first time!

We will test circuits 1 and 2 (Cooker and upstairs sockets) and fill the sheet together! This all looks very difficult initially, but it really is not as bad as it seems. The first thing to note is that you can fill in the first five columns without doing any work! These columns are for information about the circuit, not test results.

Once you have filled the left hand side of the sheet, then it is time to test the circuits!

I-ON

79

This is mine re-produced for you.

Form 4

SCHEDULE OF TEST RESULTS

Form No   /4

Contractor: *M S P*

Test Date: *8/5/06*

Signature: *Alen L*

Method of protection against indirect contact: *EEBADS*

Equipment vulnerable to testing: *DOWNLIGHTS + ALARM*

Address/Location of distribution board:

GARAGE

* Type of Supply: TN-S/TN-C-S/TT
* Ze at origin: *0.21* ohms
* PFC: *1.41* kA

Instruments

loop impedance: ....

continuity: ....

insulation: ....

RCD tester: ....

Description of Work: *NEW BUILD*

Circuit Description	Overcurrent Device		Wiring Conductors		Continuity			Insulation Resistance		P o l a r i t y	Earth Loop Imped- ance	Functional Testing		Remarks
	* Short-circuit capacity: *6* kA													
	type	Rating I_n	live	cpc	$(R_1 + R_2)$*	R_2*	R i n g	Live/ Live	Live/ Earth		Z_s	RCD time	Other	
		A	mm²	mm²	Ω	Ω	g	MΩ	MΩ		Ω	ms		
1	2	3	4	5	* 6	* 7	* 8	* 9	* 10	* 11	* 12	* 13	* 14	15
1 COOKER	B	32	6·0	2·5								✕		OUTLET NOW 2-GANG S/O CUPBOARD
2 POWER UP	B	32	2·5	1·5								✕		INC GARAGE DOOR OPERATOR

Test Results

Also, note that no rcd protection is fitted to these two circuits so I have put a cross in the "rcd time" boxes. In addition, I have put a little extra circuit information in the remarks column.

You should see now that the schedule is not so daunting because you have...

Done half of it without doing anything!

This now completes our "**LIVE**" testing of the mains. Now it is time to run through the "**DEAD**" testing of the circuit to be connected in to the consumer unit.

Continuity of "Radial" Protective Conductors
(Including equipotential bonding conductors) P69 OSG

Mains live test	Incoming polarity test
Mains live test	Prospective fault current test
Mains live test	Ext. earth loop impedance test (Ze) or eath electrode test (Ra)
Circuit dead test	Continuity of protective conductors or ring circuit test
Circuit dead test	Insulation resistance test
Circuit dead test	Circuit polarity test
Circuit connected live test	Earth loop impedance test (Zs)
Circuit connected live test	RCD trip time test

The purpose of this test on a radial circuit:

- Is to make sure the cpc at the consumer unit makes it all the way, unbroken, to the end of the circuit.

Unfortunately in all my years on the job, this is yet another neglected test. Earthing, as discussed elsewhere, vitally important. Unfortunately, many electricians tend to turn on an untested circuit and then go "searching" for an earth. This is totally unacceptable for the following reason.

The primary protection from indirect contact is EEBADS, so if you were to energize an installation with missing earths, then by definition you would have no protection from indirect contact, this is not good! It would also constitute an instant failure by a scheme inspector.

To re-iterate then, this first test is to simply make sure that the cpc that leaves the consumer unit makes it all the way, unbroken, to the end of the circuit.

Before we start out you should know that there are two different ways to do it. In the OSG they are listed as:

- Method 1 or "R1+R2 test"
- Method 2 or "Wander lead test"

We will now look at these separately.

Test method 1

There is a picture of this test method on P68 OSG. All you need to do is pop a link in at the consumer unit between live and earth and take a reading at ALL points on the DEAD circuit under test. The reading is taken between live and the cpc. The Institute call the live wire "R1" and the earth wire or cpc "R2". The highest reading on a circuit would be put in the relevant column in the test schedule. On an IEE schedule, this would be column six (R1+R2).

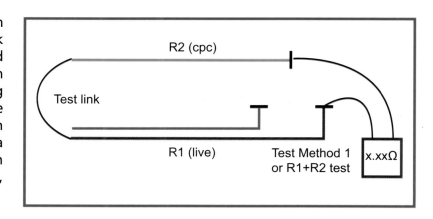

Test method 2

With this method, you have a long wander lead connected to the cpc at the consumer unit. You then go to all points on the circuit under test and check for continuity. The highest reading would then go into column seven on the schedule of test results (R2).

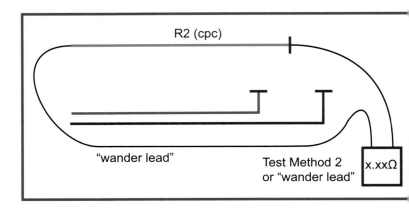

So then, which is the easy option for you when continuity testing? The truth of the matter is that tes method 2 never really gets used. There is a good reason for this and all will be revealed further on in thi chapter. Without knowing why though, it can be seen that R1+R2 testing is far easier as you do not need wander lead. The wander lead is effectively the live or R1 that runs along side the cpc inside the twin an earth cable, wherever it goes.

The only time you have to use method 2, shown above, is to perform a continuity check on main an supplementary equipotential bonding conductors. On an EIC, **p130 OSG**, there is no box for recording reading for these cables. It has a tick box titled "Connection verified". Electricians tend not to measure th cable. They mearly install it, connect it and tick the box! This, in my opinion, is fair enough. An electricia will argue that it can be seen to be connected at both ends and if it was severed part way through its run, a seven strands of the conductor would have to be broken at the same point with no visible external damage As the regulations say "so far as is reasonably practicable!"
The only time you would be obliged to measure an equipotential bonding conductor would be on a jo where you are adding a new circuit to an existing installation. If the existing main equipotential bondin conductor was not visible throughout its entire length, then it would be prudent to prove its continuity Another example could be where you are to perform a periodic report on an existing installation an once again you cannot see the bonding conductor throughout its length. The test would prove that th conductor is in-tact. It must be said now, that until you are experienced, periodic reporting is really outsid your scope.

With this stated I shall now demonstrate test method 1 or "R1+R2" testing to you.

he first job you need to do is set your meter on its "low Ohm" setting. The next task then, is to "zero or null" the test leads. You have to do this so you do not end up with artificially high readings due to reading the leads all the time. Any modern unit has this facility. If your tester cannot "zero or null" then you need to take the reading like me here and subtract this reading from your circuit readings. My meter is nulled here as I have a reading of 0.00Ω with the leads connected together.

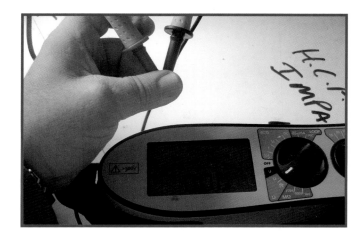

our OSG tells you to put a link in between live and earth but the job can be made easier still. Before terminating the cable in the board, I have simply stripped the cable and twisted the live and earth together. I just need to go to the other end of this cooker cable now and...

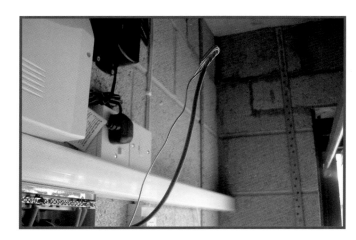

take a reading at all points on the circuit. The kitchen fitter asked me to put a double socket on the end of the cable rather than a traditional cooker outlet plate. Also, in this picture you can see my "magic plug" in use. This is simply a 13A plug top with holes drilled in the back so I can get the test probes in! This is handy if the socket manufacturer has shutters on his sockets that are hard to disable.

Here you can see the reading of 0.21Ω, which I got from the cooker outlet. As per the OSG, I have checked for continuity at "all points" on the circuit. I did have a slightly lower reading at the wall switch but the highest reading recorded here is what will be entered on the sheet.

Form 4
SCHEDULE OF TEST RESULTS

Form No   /4

Contractor: M S P
Test Date: 8/5/06
Signature ....Alen L....
Method of protection against indirect contact: EEBADS
Equipment vulnerable to testing: DOWNLIGHTS + ALARM.

Address/Location of distribution board:
GARAGE

* Type of Supply: TN-S/TN-C-S/TT
* Ze at origin: 0.21 ohms
* PFC: 1.41 kA

Instruments
loop impedance: ....
continuity: ....
insulation: ....
RCD tester: ....

Description of Work: NEW BUILD

Circuit Description	Overcurrent Device * Short-circuit capacity: ...6..kA		Wiring Conductors		Test Results									Remarks
	type	Rating I_n	live	cpc	Continuity			Insulation Resistance		Polarity	Earth Loop Imped-ance	Functional Testing		
					$(R_1 + R_2)$*	R_2*	Ring	Live/Live	Live/Earth		Z_s	RCD time	Other	
		A	mm²	mm²	Ω	Ω	g	MΩ	MΩ		Ω	ms		
1	2	3	4	5	*6	*7	*8	*9	*10	*11	*12	*13	*14	15
1 COOKER	B	32	6·0	2·5	0·21	X	X					✕		OUTLET NOW 2-GANG S/O CUPBOARD
2 POWER UP	B	32	2·5	1·5								✕		INC GARAGE DOOR OPERATOR

And here is the recorded maximum figure of 0.21Ω, which I have entered into the "R1+R2" column on the schedule.
And yes, it really is as simple as that! I have also put crosses into columns seven and eight.
The reasons for these crosses are:

- Column 7. As explained above, when performing a continuity test on a circuit you use one or other of the test methods, not both. I have not done a wander lead test so a cross goes in this column.

- Column 8. The cooker circuit under test is a radial circuit and not a ring, so I can put a cross in here as well.

I-ON

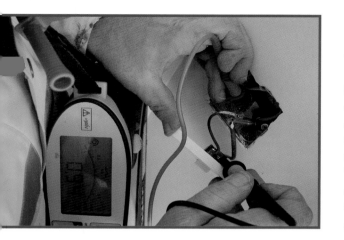

Before we move on, I shall give you another tip for R1+ R2 testing. When you second fix an installation, only screw back the sockets. The reason should now be obvious. What is the point of screwing a switch back only to unscrew it in order to perform a continuity test!

Also as you test each point , final fix it back before moving on. It will act as insurance to show that you did not forget to test anything!

This picture shows me, in action again, performing a continuity test on one of the lighting circuits. One probe is on the back of the metal switch box and the other can be seen on a switch terminal

Continuity of ring final circuit conductors protective conductors
P69 OSG

Mains live test	Incoming polarity test
Mains live test	Prospective fault current test
Mains live test	Ext. earth loop impedance test (Ze) or eath electrode test (Ra)
Circuit dead test	Continuity of protective conductors or ring circuit test
Circuit dead test	Insulation resistance test
Circuit dead test	Circuit polarity test
Circuit connected live test	Earth loop impedance test (Zs)
Circuit connected live test	RCD trip time test

The purpose of this test on a ring circuit is:

- To prove that the ring circuit is in fact a true ring and not "bridged" or "open" somewhere.

The text of the OSG describes a three part test. We shall cover it also. First we will do the theory and then do the job for real!

Step1

Switch your tester to its "low Ohms" setting. Next you must "zero or null" the instrument. These procedures are the same as shown in the previous continuity testing above. Take an "end to end" reading of the three ring conductors (L, N & E). The figures shown here are the actual figures I got for the upstairs ring on our project.

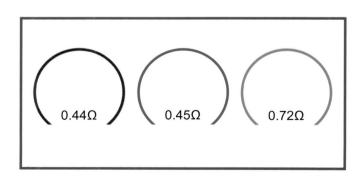

0.44Ω   0.45Ω   0.72Ω

The first thing to notice here is that:

- The live and neutral figures are almost identical.
- The cpc reading is higher.

This is quite correct as the circuit is wired in 2.5/1.5 mm twin and earth cable. The live and neutrals are the same size so a similar resistance readings for these conductors is correct.

The cpc is a smaller cable. In line with Ohm's law then it must be a higher reading because it is a smaller wire. What we need to know now is if it is the right reading.
There is a method of working out if it is correct. It is mentioned at the top of **p70 OSG**.

- The ratio is stated as 2.5/1.5=1.67

In other words if the cpc is around 1.67 times the resistance of the live and neutral readings, then the circuit has passed its first test.
Our ring example above gives an estimate of cpc resistance of

- 0.44Ω (live loop above) X 1.67(stated ratio) =0.73Ω (estimate of cpc reading).

Our actual cpc reading of 0.72Ω is more or less perfect so we can proceed. **P70 OSG** states that the ring readings should be within 0.05Ω of each other.   If you were to get bad figures at this stage, then you either have a wire out of a socket (infinite reading) or loose wire (high reading).

Step 2

The next task is to prove that the ring really is a ring. You do this by:

- Cross-connecting the incoming live to the outgoing neutral at the consumer unit and visa versa.
- Work out what projected reading you should then get at all points on the ring.
- Take a reading between live and neutrals at all points on the ring to check.

This is explained and illustrated on **p70- 71 OSG**. I have also reproduced this task in my diagram at the top of **p88**.
After the cross-connection of the lives and neutrals, you must now work out what your projected reading should be. Referring to the loop figures above, our socket reading should be:

$$\frac{\text{Live loop + neutral loop}}{4} = \frac{0.44+ 0.45}{4} = \frac{0.89}{4} = 0.22\Omega$$

You would be quite right now to be saying *"So where does he get the "4 bit" from?"*
This is easily explained in the following diagrams.

This demonstration is using our live and neutral loops from the upstairs ring circuit. The meter shows the total of the two readings. This then follows ohms law. *The longer the wire, the higher the resistance.*

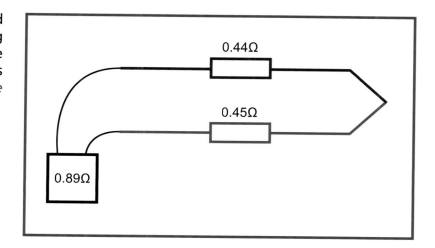

Now I have connected together the free ends of my loop and measured again. The reading has quartered in value.

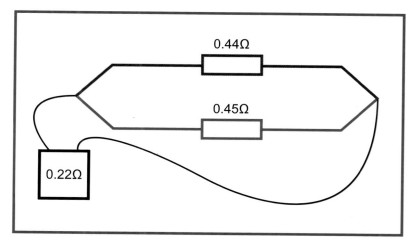

The technical reason for this is that copper resistance is proportional to length and inversely proportional to the cross sectional area. To put it into more simple terms, please look at the diagrams again...

- In the second diagram the wire has now become half the length and twice as fat!

And following on from Ohm's Law...

- Half the length means half the resistance
- Twice as fat means half the resistance

And as you may remember from school...

- A half multiplied by a half is a quarter!

This is the same diagram of the ring as above, but now I have put it into a form that looks more like our wiring installation. The lives and neutrals are now cross-connected at the consumer unit. You can also see a test meter connected at a socket to take a measurement. The reading measured should be close to the calculated reading.

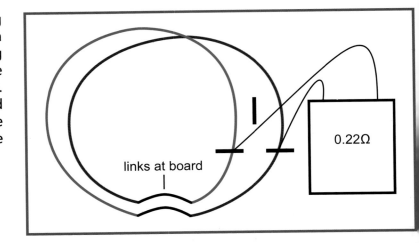

Step 3

We are nearly finished now, all that is left to do now is:

- Cross-connect the lives and earths at the consumer unit
- Work out our projected reading at each point on the ring
- Take a reading at each point on the ring

We now disconnect the neutrals and connect in their place the two cpcs. Again, using our project ring readings above, you should obtain a reading of around:

$$\frac{\text{Live loop+ cpc loop}}{4} = \frac{0.44+ 0.72}{4} = \frac{1.16}{4} = 0.29\Omega$$

Here is a diagram of the ring as it would be in the house. The lives and cpcs are now cross-connected at the consumer unit. You can also see a test meter connected at a socket to take a measurement. The reading measured should be close to the calculated reading.

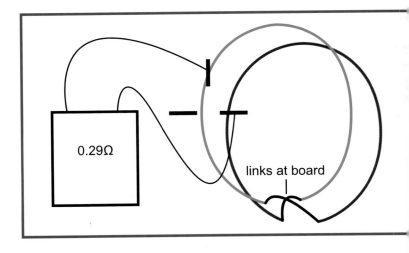

Before I move on to demonstrate the test for real there are a couple of points I need to discuss:

- Remember when doing steps 2 and 3 if you have any spurs off your ring these will give higher readings.

- When you cross-connect at the consumer unit, it is possible to connect the wrong lives to the wrong neutrals and earths. If you get the conductors "mixed up" (so the drawings above end up looking like a long circular sausage!), you will get a very low reading near to the mains. It will climb as you go round the ring and come back down as you get back towards the mains. If you do this, you will definitely know about it!

The last thing to discuss now is where you put all these figures!

- Step 1 test. Record in relevant columns, if provided on your schedule. On an IEE schedule **(p132 OSG)** there is nowhere to record these figures.

- Step 2 tests. These readings are never recorded, only noted to make sure the ring is healthy.

- Step 3 tests. The very highest live to earth reading recorded is put into the "R1+R2" column. On the IEE schedule, **(p132 OSG)** this is column 6.

Please do not worry too much about ring testing. Many electricians do not know how to do it properly and my explanation has taken quite a lot of reading! When doing it for real it is a lot simpler once you get in to the swing of it! We will run through it now.

Performing step 1

I have once again put my tester on its "low ohm" setting and checked that it is "zeroing" correctly. I have measured the live-live loop and I am now doing the neutral-neutral loop. I just need to measure the cpc-cpc loop now and we will be ready to do step 2. The figures are scribbled onto my rough schedule pinned on the wall.

On to step 2

As with the cooker test above, it is best to do the cross connection with long tails. (After testing, you can terminate the conductors in properly). I have cross-connected the live and neutral loops now and I am ready to "walk" the upstairs of the installation.

To recap now, the test 1 end-end loop readings were:

- Live   0.44Ω
- Neutral   0.45Ω

Therefore, at each point, I should be getting a reading of around:

- $\dfrac{0.44+0.45}{4} = 0.22Ω$

All readings recorded were around this figure. It is a little higher than we calculated but nothing to worry about. Remember the ring is connected into the back of this socket, so I will also be reading the resistance of the socket itself and socket switch.

Remember, there is nowhere to record these figures, they are for checking only. Don't forget, if you are struggling to get your test probes in like me, then you need to get out your "magic plug". Once all the sockets are read that's step 2 completed.

On to step 3

You can see that I have disconnected the neutrals here and substituted them with the cpcs. Again, before I go upstairs I need to do a quick check to see what my projected figure will be. That way I will be able to spot any problems immediately.

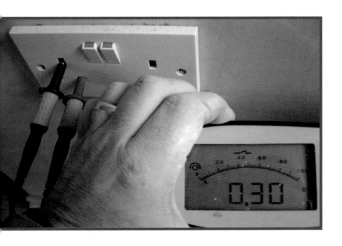

To recap again, my test 1 end-end loop readings were:

- Live   0.44Ω
- Cpc   0.72Ω

Therefore, I should be getting around:

- $\dfrac{0.44+0.72}{4} = 0.29Ω$

Once again, I got excellent readings as I "walked" the circuit under test. Using the same reasoning as step 2, if they had been a little higher than this I would not have worried. Nevertheless, they were all around the 0.29 and 0.30Ω mark, so the job was considered a success story.

- One more thing to bear in mind is that when you install 2.5/1.5mm²-twin and earth cable for a ring, even with it cross-connected correctly, you may see the readings varying slightly when doing the step 3 test. This is because the live and cpc rings you are testing are different cross sectional areas. Do not worry about this, as it is normal. Some times it makes a difference of up to 0.05Ω. This ring did not suffer with this trait. It all depends on how the circuit is wired and how the sockets are spread around it.

The final task is to record my highest step 3 reading as the test R1+R2 for the circuit.

Here are the final figures for my ring circuit.
Again, I have also filled columns 7 & 8. The reasons are:

- Column 7 I have done a ring test and not a "wander lead" test, therefore a cross goes here.

- Column 8. We have proved a healthy ring here, so we can tick this one!

Form 4
SCHEDULE OF TEST RESULTS   Form No   /4

Contractor: M S P
Test Date: 8/5/06
Signature
Method of protection against indirect contact: EEBADS
Equipment vulnerable to testing: DOWNLIGHTS + ALARM

Address/Location of distribution board:
GARAGE

* Type of Supply: TN-S/TN-C-S/TT
* Ze at origin: 0.21 ohms
* PFC: 1.41 kA

Instruments
loop impedance:
continuity:
insulation:
RCD tester:

Description of Work: NEW BUILD

Circuit Description	Overcurrent Device * Short-circuit capacity: ...6..kA		Wiring Conductors		Test Results										Remarks
					Continuity			Insulation Resistance		P o l a r i t y	Earth Loop Imped- ance	Functional Testing			
	type	Rating I$_n$	live	cpc	(R$_1$ + R$_2$)*	R$_2$*	R i n g	Live/ Live	Live/ Earth		Z$_s$	RCD time	Other	
		A	mm²	mm²	Ω	Ω		MΩ	MΩ		Ω	ms		
1	2	3	4	5	* 6	* 7	* 8	* 9	* 10	* 11	* 12	* 13	* 14	15
1 COOKER	B	32	6.0	2.5	0.21	✗	✗					✗		OUTLET NOW 2-GANG S/O CUPBOARD)
2 POWER UP	B	32	2.5	1.5	0.30	✗	✓					✗		INC GARAGE DOOR OPERATOR

As you can see it takes a lot longer to explain this test than it actually takes to do it! I will accept that it takes more time than a radial circuit, as you have to walk the circuit twice but is still quick and simple. Notice that the "dreaded" schedule is rapidly filling!

As a final thought on ring testing, you may be saying," Why does he do this elaborate three part test to prove this ring, when he has wired it, and *knows* it is a ring?" There is a good reason why, which I shall come to later in this part of the book.

This completes the continuity testing for ring and radial circuits now. We shall now proceed to the next part of circuit testing procedure.

Insulation resistance testing
P72 OSG

Mains live test	Incoming polarity test
Mains live test	Prospective fault current test
Mains live test	Ext. earth loop impedance test (Ze) or eath electrode test (Ra)
Circuit dead test	Continuity of protective conductors or ring circuit test
Circuit dead test	Insulation resistance test
Circuit dead test	Circuit polarity test
Circuit connected live test	Earth loop impedance test (Zs)
Circuit connected live test	RCD trip time test

Following your continuity or ring test, you are now ready to perform an insulation resistance test on your circuit.

The reason for this test is:

- To prove that the circuit's insulation is intact with no short circuits or leaks.

A similar analogy could be drawn from a man who installs a sprinkler system in a building. The pipe install obviously should not leak and is always pressure tested before the ceilings and flooring go in. Usually, if a system is to say operate at four bar of pressure, it will be tested at say six bar for a couple of hours. If it does not leak after this, when it is up and running (with the lower working pressure) it will never leak. And so, it is the same with our circuits.
Yet again, this is another badly neglected test performed by electricians. This is a test, which must be performed before a circuit is energized. Sadly, most electricians energize a circuit and if it goes "bang" then they get the insulation tester out!

Looking at table 10.1 on **p73 OSG**, our 230V circuits (bottom row of table) are "pressure tested" to a value of 500V. When we do this, we measure the resistance across the insulation. The table tells us that the minimum resistance is 0.5MΩ. Note this is a "big" M and signifies "a million" so our minimum allowed reading is a half a million ohms. Also, the term MΩ is pronounced as "meg-ohm"
In addition, in the text we are told that a reading of below 2MΩ will require investigation. When doing this task on new work your readings should be nowhere down near these readings if your circuit is fault free. As before, we will do a little theory and then do the job for real.
On any circuit you only need to do three tests, they are:

- Between live and earth.
- Between neutral and earth.
- Between live and neutral.

You can do these three tests in any order, though this is my preferred order.
Caution must be exercised when doing the third test. There is no problem when testing socket outlets. You simply make sure nothing is plugged in! However there can be difficulties when testing circuits with electronics or non-removable loads fitted. You may damage something by putting 500V across it. The secret is to think before you press the button!

It is best to look at diagrams now with explanations. This will help explain the text of the OSG.

Socket outlet circuits (radials or rings)

Nice easy test this one!
Make sure nothing is plugged in and perform all three tests listed above.

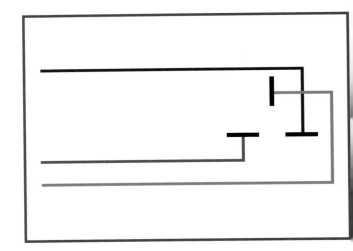

Lighting circuits with "bulbs"

Close all switches and remove lamps.
You would then perform all three tests listed above. Obviously having the switch "open" would mean that you were not testing the live side all the way to the lamp holder, so make sure the switches are closed. If the circuit you are wiring is controlled by a two-way switch, do not forget to operate both switches and repeat on the live to earth test. If you do not do this test and one of the two-way strappers had an insulation fault on it, it could go "bang" when you switch on or off when energised. This is not good!

Lighting circuits with selv down lights or sodium outside lights

This is where the problems start now!
If you do the live to neutral test as above you would get a short circuit between live and neutral with the switch closed. This is because when you remove the lamp, the transformer or choke unit is still connected! It is un-realistic to disconnect all the transformers as you could declare the circuit fault free and then cause a fault when you "squash" the wiring reconnecting the transformers.
Though not ideal, we are allowed to leave the local switches open for the live to neutral test.

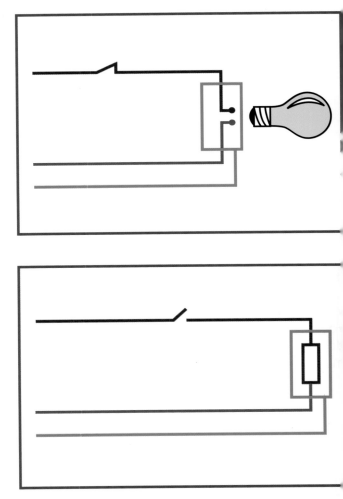

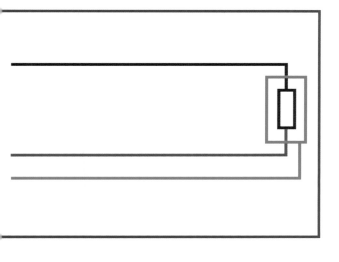

Circuits with no switch such as pir controllers

In this type of circuit, you could disconnect the item, do all the tests and reconnect as above. Also, as mentioned above you could cause an insulation fault when performing this disconnection and reconnection operation. OSG tells us we can abandon the live to neutral test. Therefore, we need only test:

- Live to earth
- Neutral to earth

On the certificate, we can record that we did not do the live to neutral test by either putting a cross in the relevant box or writing "LIM" denoting a limitation of test.

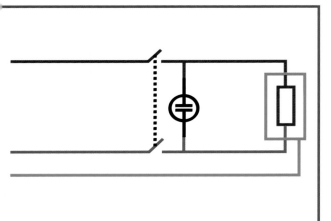

Circuits with double pole switches and/or neon indicators

This is the type of switch that usually supplies fixed loads, such as immersion heaters, central heating systems and cookers. It is a d.p. (double pole) switch, in other words the live and neutral are switched together at the same time. Also, I have shown this switch with a neon indicator. That is the round thing you see here! On this type of circuit the easiest way to test is to:

- **Close the switch** and test live to earth and neutral to earth.

- **Open the switch** and test between live and neutral.

If you wire central heating or say air conditioning for a living, this is definitely the test method for you.

We will now do some insulation resistance testing on our project. By the way, when you look at the photos you will see the symbol ">" on the instrument display. This simply means "greater than". Electricians do not generally call this work insulation resistance testing, but shorten the name to "IR testing". Even more commonly, it is called megger testing or "meggering" after the famous manufacturer.

First job to do is to prove the tester is working! I have set the unit to its 500V MΩ insulation testing setting and I am pressing the test button. I have the crocodile clips apart here so I should get a maximum reading. I am reading a resistance of greater than 299MΩ between the clips. Yes, that is greater than 299,000,000Ω! This is a very high figure and shows that air is a good insulator!

Now I have put the crocodile clips together and re-measured. The reading of 0.00MΩ now indicates a dead short. This confirms the tester is fine and now I can go testing the insulation resistance of our two project circuits.

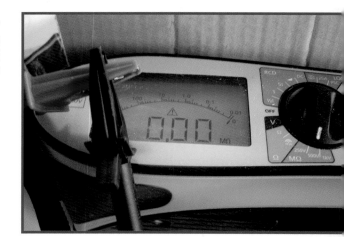

This first insulation test is being done on the cooker circuit, which we tested for earth continuity some time back.
Let's recap the list of IR tests required:

- Test 1 live to earth
- Test 2 neutral to earth
- Test 3 live to neutral

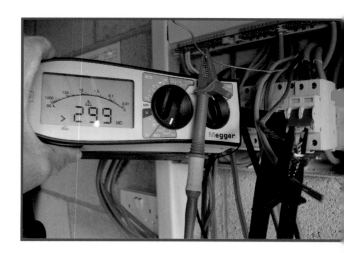

If you look at this picture and the test order, I have the cpc in the red clip. I have the live and neutral "together" in the black clip. This means I am performing tests one and two at the same time. The reading shown is greater than 299 MΩ, so then does it pass?

Well, **p73 OSG** tells us the *minimum* reading allowed is:

- 0.5 MΩ Below this is a "fail"
- 2.0 MΩ Below this "requires investigation"

We got a reading of greater than 299MΩ, which is a good "pass". Incidentally, this reading was the same as our meter test with the crocodile clips in thin air. This then proves our cooker circuit definitely has no insulation defects.
An electrician would use the term "clear" to describe this reading.
The final job now is to do a test between live and neutral.

I am now performing the live to neutral test on the cooker circuit and I have found a problem. I have a reading of 0.26MΩ.
The table on **p73 OSG** tells us that the minimum IR must be greater than 0.5MΩ. Experience alone will give a pointer as to what is wrong.

- If you get a reading of around "a quarter of a megohm", it will always be a neon indicator you are reading.

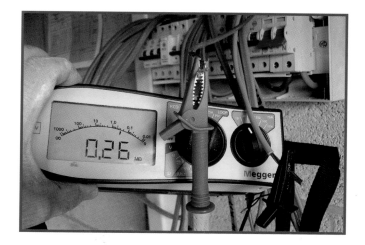

f you can see the switch as you press the test button, you will see that the tester will actually be lighting he neon! Remember you are pumping 500V down the circuit! I went to the kitchen and switched off he cooker isolator. When I returned and retested the reading was a "clear" >299MΩ.

There is just one thing to mention here before I write the test figures in. You would be surprised how many electricians do this test with switches and sockets not screwed back to the wall. This obviously is a waste off time as a circuit could "pass" an IR test and then you could trap a wire when screwing back a switch or socket. However, if you have been following this book up to now, then it should not be an ssue as I told you to screw the switches back after continuity testing!

Before I fill the test sheet, I am going to do an IR test on that upstairs ring I continuity tested previously.

As you have seen me doing on the cooker circuit, I am firstly testing live and neutral, together in the red clip at the same time, to earth.
The reading again is clear. As with the cooker I have left the tails nice and long so they are easier to work with.

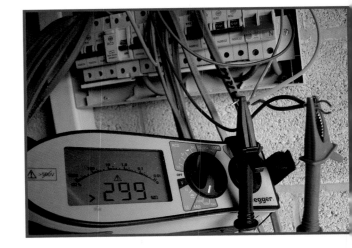

The final test on the upstairs ring circuit is between live and neutral. Once again, a very high reading indicates there are no insulation defects. One thing to note about ring IR testing is that you can test any of the wires, when performing this task. You have already proved that both lives, for instance, end up at the consumer unit in front of you.

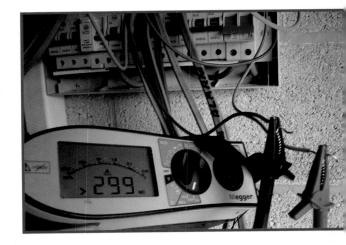

All readings can now go on the schedule and I can move on to the other circuits. Once I have IR tested all the circuits, then I will finally dress in and terminate all conductors, at last!

Form 4

SCHEDULE OF TEST RESULTS

Form No   /4

Contractor: ....M S P.............................

Test Date: ....8/5/06........................

Signature ......*Alen Lylu*.........................

Method of protection against indirect contact: ......EEBADS............

Equipment vulnerable to testing: ......DOWNLIGHTS + ALARM..........

Address/Location of distribution board:

......................GARAGE..............................

* Type of Supply: TN-S/TN-C-S/TT
* Ze at origin: O.2.I. ohms
* PFC: I.4.I. kA

Instruments

loop impedance: ....

continuity: ....

insulation: ....

RCD tester: ....

Description of Work: ......NEW   BUILD.............................

Circuit Description	Overcurrent Device		Wiring Conductors		Continuity			Insulation Resistance		P o l a r i t y	Earth Loop Imped-ance	Functional Testing		Remarks
	* Short-circuit capacity: ...6..kA										Z_s	RCD time	Other	
	type	Rating I_n	live	cpc	$(R_1 + R_2)$*	R_2*	R i n g	Live/ Live	Live/ Earth					
		A	mm²	mm²	Ω	Ω		MΩ	MΩ		Ω	ms		
1	2	3	4	5	*6	*7	*8	*9	*10	*11	*12	*13	*14	15
1 COOKER	B	32	6.0	2.5	0.21	X	X	>299	>299			X		OUTLET NOW 2-GANG S/O CUPBOARD
2 POWER UP	B	32	2.5	1.5	0.30	X	✓	>299	>299			X		INC GARAGE DOOR OPERATOR

Here is the up to date schedule. I have filled in the IR columns. The columns that cover this test are nine and ten, and are titled:

- Column 9. Live to live reading
- Column 10 Live to earth reading

Do not worry, they have not made a mistake! In regulations terminology a live conductor means live or neutral! That is why the technically correct term for a live conductor is "phase". On this form then the lowest of the live to earth and neutral to earth readings goes in the L-E column. The live to neutral reading goes in the L-L column.

Before we move on, there are just a few IR testing issues that I want to cover.

The first is illustrated here. The OSG tells us that we must IR test selv circuits. Looking again at table 10.2 **p73 OSG** we now test at 250V between the input and output of a selv transformer to check for leakage between the two windings. Here I am demonstrating the test on a bell transformer. I have one probe on the 240V side and the other on the V side of the transformer. The minimum reading allowed is 0.25MΩ and our reading is >99.9MΩ so once again this is declared fault free. On this tester's 250V setting the maximum reading is >99.9MΩ).

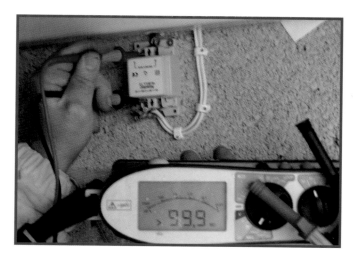

The same IR test should also be done on all the down lighting transformers. The minimum reading must again be greater than 0.25MΩ. It would obviously be easier to test lighting transformers **before** you install them (on the bench).

To be honest it is a test that you never see electricians doing even though they should! In their defence, the transformers should be tested at the factory.

The next issue I want to cover is the IR testing of our project lighting circuits. On our project, I had a mix of normal tungsten lamp lighting and selv lighting. Looking again at the methods of testing above and just to reiterate:

- On the "normal" tungsten lighting, I removed all lamps and closed the switches controlling these lamps
- On selv lighting, I left lamps in and opened the local switches
- And I did not forget to operate the two-way switches on the live to earth test

I then performed the IR tests:

- Live to earth
- Neutral to earth
- Live to neutral

I would now like to cover a myth that floats around the electrical industry. A lot of electricians simply wire a circuit and switch on without testing. Then if it goes "bang", the insulation resistance tester comes out! However if there is a fault between neutral and earth it does not go bang. This is because as you now know, the two conductors are connected together at the supply sub-station. This myth then runs along the lines of

MYTH   *What's the big deal with neutral to earth faults, they don't harm anyone!*

This is one of the more disturbing myths that I have heard over the years. It is one of the most dangerous of all practices. The following diagrams will explain why.

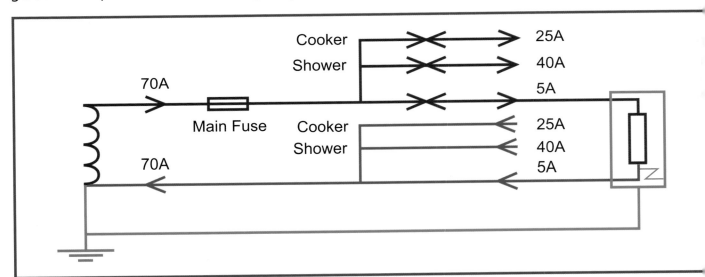

This TN-S installation has a neutral to earth fault on the lighting circuit. This is shown as the red zig-zag line. An "electrician" has fitted a new light recently and not performed an IR test on the circuit. It Sunday dinnertime and the cooker is on and one of the teenagers is in the shower. If you follow th arrows, you should be able to see how the 70A coming in on the live splits up and returns back dow the neutral. Everything is fine until...

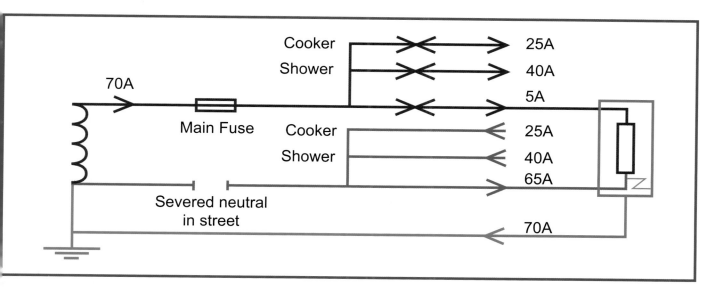

..The neutral severs in the street. If this house was insulation fault free the house would simply stop working. Not good, but safe. On this installation, however, there is still a return path via the neutral to earth fault. Again looking at the route of the currents, the neutral of the lighting circuit is now carrying 65A and the cpc 70A. This circuit is wired in 1.0mm2 or 1.5mm2 twin and earth cable which are only rated to carry around 10 or 15A respectively. The cable will burn and possibly set the house alight. Even worse, note that the breakers will not trip as they cannot "see" a fault. If you think this is rare, think again. In twenty five years I have attended five of these incidents. The moral of this example is not to fiddle your paperwork because you are late for another appointment. Now you are aware of the risk, it does not bear thinking about to not perform IR testing.

This concludes the insulation testing of these circuits. I have "cracked on" and tested the rest of the installation. It was declared fault free, thank goodness! Usually on these type of jobs, it is always in the back of one's mind that a joiner has put a nail through a cable when fitting his skirting boards, but alas not this time!

CIRCUIT POLARITY TESTING P78 OSG

Mains live test	Incoming polarity test
Mains live test	Prospective fault current test
Mains live test	Ext. earth loop impedance test (Ze) or eath electrode test (Ra)
Circuit dead test	Continuity of protective conductors or ring circuit test
Circuit dead test	Insulation resistance test
Circuit dead test	Circuit polarity test
Circuit connected live test	Earth loop impedance test (Zs)
Circuit connected live test	RCD trip time test

The purpose of this test is to prove that:

- All single pole switches and beakers/fuses are fitted in the live conductor.

- Edison screw lamp holders have their live pin connected to the centre contact.
  (Unless of course it is one of those newer all plastic models, in which case it does not matter which way round it is connected).

- All sockets are connected correctly.

To illustrate the importance of this test please look at the two diagrams.

Here our "victim" has switched off a lounge light fitting. He is replacing a blown lamp. He has stuck his finger into the empty lampholder. However, he is safe, as the live side of the lampholder is not connected to the live side of the supply.

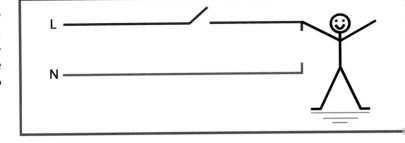

This time though, the circuit has been wired with a reverse polarity fault. The light will switch on and off normally. This misleads our "victim" to believe the circuit is safe, giving the appearance of being "off" when it is still, in fact live. Not good at all!

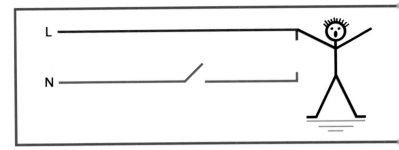

You can see now that this test is of utmost importance, just as all the previous ones.

Vell if you take a quick look at the text on **p78 OSG**, congratulations, you have already done this ask! And the reasons for this?

- **On the mains.** The very first task that I undertook when testing was the safe isolation of the incoming supply. I stated then that this was a good time to check the incoming polarity, which I did. The incoming polarity check is mentioned half way down **p78 OSG.**

- **On radial circuits.** When I was performing my R1+R2 continuity tests, I was proving that the "live" wire at all points on the circuit under test was in fact "live". In addition, at light fittings my R1+R2 reading disappears when I open the local switches. This is shown on **p77 OSG**. This proves that the switch is in the R1 or live conductor. If the switch was in the neutral, switching it on and off would have no effect on the R1+R2 measurement. Way back on **p82** I said there was a good reason not to perform "R2" or the "wander lead" method when performing continuity tests. The reason is that it **cannot** prove polarity.

- **On ring circuits.** When I performed the three-part ring circuit test, I have automatically proved that the sockets have correct polarity. This is stated at the bottom of **p70 OSG**. Going back to the ring test section, if a socket on a ring was wired "live and neutral reversed" then you would get no reading on the step three test, as you would be,

1. Attempting to measure between live and earth.
2. Actually measuring across neutral and earth. (Try drawing this out for yourself).

As for polarity then, I always tell my students in this way:

"If the wiring is proved right coming in and proved right going out, when you put it together it will be right!"

Now looking at the schedule of test results, as we do each R1+R2 or ring test we can automatically put tick in that circuit's polarity box! So now you are performing two tests at once, excellent news for the hard pressed tradesman! Here is my updated sheet.

	Form 4													Form No /4

SCHEDULE OF TEST RESULTS

Contractor: *M S P*
Address/Location of distribution board:
Instruments

Test Date: *8/5/06*
loop impedance: ....
GARAGE
* Type of Supply: TN-S/TN-C-S/~~TT~~
continuity: ....

Signature *Alen Lh*
* Ze at origin: *0.21* ohms
insulation: ....

Method of protection against indirect contact: *EEBADS*
* PFC: *1.41* kA
RCD tester: ....

Equipment vulnerable to testing: *DOWN LIGHTS + ALARM*

Description of Work: *NEW BUILD*

Circuit Description	Overcurrent Device * Short-circuit capacity: ...6..kA		Wiring Conductors		Test Results							Earth Loop Imped-ance	Functional Testing		Remarks
					Continuity			Insulation Resistance		P o l a r i t y					
	type	Rating I_n	live	cpc	$(R_1 + R_2)*$	R_2*	R i n g	Live/ Live	Live/ Earth		Z_s	RCD time	Other	
		A	mm²	mm²	Ω	Ω	Ω	MΩ	MΩ		Ω	ms		
1	2	3	4	5	*6	*7	*8	*9	*10	*11	*12	*13	*14	15
1 COOKER	B	32	6.0	2.5	0.21	X	X	>299	>299	✓		X		OUTLET NOW 2-GANG S/O CUPBOARD
2 POWER UP	B	32	2.5	1.5	0.30	X	✓	>299	>299	✓		X		INC GARAGE DOOR OPERATOR

To put closure on this section now, a cautionary tale. A few years ago, I was involved with a job where a socket was wired wrong, but passed its tests. The circuit in question was a radial circuit feeding an all insulated socket. An "electrician" had wired the socket with the live and earth connections reversed. This socket promptly passed its R1+R2 test and its insulation test. It was then energised. If someone had plugged in a metal appliance, they would have been electrocuted from it! (Get some coloured pens and try drawing it out for yourself.) To conclude this point then:

- Even though you have proved polarity correct on a circuit during R1+R2 testing,
  please perform a quick live polarity check at one point as soon as it is energised.

It just goes to show that the testing regime is not perfect. This problem does not generally affect lighting or ring final circuits. Therefore, the polarity correct "tick" on our newly tested cooker circuit above is provisional and will be finally double-checked when energised.

This now concludes the "dead testing of the circuits". The circuits can now be terminated into the consumer unit and be energised. We can then proceed with the live testing.

EARTH FAULT LOOP IMPEDANCE TESTING P79 OSG

Mains live test	Incoming polarity test
Mains live test	Prospective fault current test
Mains live test	Ext. earth loop impedance test (Ze) or eath electrode test (Ra)
Circuit dead test	Continuity of protective conductors or ring circuit test
Circuit dead test	Insulation resistance test
Circuit dead test	Circuit polarity test
Circuit connected live test	Earth loop impedance test (Zs)
Circuit connected live test	RCD trip time test

The next thing we need to do now is record the earth loop impedance or Zs of the circuit that you have just connected.

The reason for this test is to prove that:

- The value of earth loop impedance at the end of the circuit is sufficiently low, so in the event of an earth fault the fuse or breaker protecting the circuit will disconnect within its maximum disconnection time.

On **p76**, you may remember that we recorded the installation's Ze. This was the *external earth loop impedance*. We did this to make sure that there was a true electrical earth to the property from the external supply.

Here we are going to measure and record the circuit Zs. Zs is short for,

- *System* earth loop impedance.

From **p19**, you may remember that I said a system is,

- "From the sub-station to the playstation". In other words, all the way down the street from the supply all the way through your wiring to say a lounge light.

Searching within the text within **p79 OSG**, there are two ways of getting this Zs figure:

- Direct measurement (Done with the circuit Live).
- The "add up" method (Done with the circuit Live or Dead).

We shall look at these now, one at a time. Again, we shall cover theory first and practice second!

Direct measurement

Here you do exactly as described. You take a meter and switch it to its earth loop impedance setting. You then go to the circuit and take a "live" measurement between live and earth. You record this reading in column twelve (Earth loop impedance Zs) of the schedule of test results. The reading is taken at the place you recorded your highest R1+R2 reading during continuity testing.

The "add up" method

When the fifteenth edition of the regulations appeared in 1981, it carried a lot of new and controversial thinking. One of the equations that appeared in there was:

- $Zs = Ze + (R1 + R2)$

Way back on **p10-11**, we were discussing the electrical terms of resistance(R) and impedance (Z). On those pages, I stated that the terms are very similar and can be treated as the same.
Well this is the proof!
This is pretty exciting, as you may have spotted that previously you have measured:

- **Ze during your "external earth loop impedance test"**
- **R1+R2 during your "continuity" or "ring" tests**

Therefore you can just "add them up" and put the resultant number into the Zs box!

So, the next question should be, "Which method shall I use?" Well you can use either. I like the easy life so generally I use the addition method. It is also worth mentioning that if you did a direct measurement on say a light switch, you *could* trap a wire when screwing it back and cause an insulation fault. However, a consultant or self-certification scheme inspector will accept either figure obtained. The other thing mentioned on **p79 OSG** is that the direct measured figure will generally be lower than the added up figure. The reason for this is when you measure live, you may also be measuring those gas and water pipes of the installation. These are known as parallel paths and are explained on **p77**.

Now we shall do some testing and paperwork.

On the project bungalow, we have been testing the upstairs ring and cooker circuit.
I used the addition method for the Zs figures for these and all the circuits.

However, here I am demonstrating a direct measurement on the TV amplifier socket fitted in the garage. The tester is on its "loop" setting and I have simply plugged it in. At the top of the instrument's display panel is a "live" polarity checker. Correct polarity is shown.
If you look at the finished EIC for this installation at the end of this part, you will see that the figures for this direct measurement and my addition method (Zs=Ze+R1+R2) are very similar.

Form 4

SCHEDULE OF TEST RESULTS

Form No   /4

Contractor: ...M S P.........................

Address/Location of distribution board:

Instruments

Test Date: ..8/5/06..........

................G A R A G E.................

* Type of Supply: TN-S/TN-C-S/TT

loop impedance: ....

Signature ....

* Ze at origin: 0.21.ohms

continuity: ....

Method of protection against indirect contact: ......EEBADS.........

* PFC: 1.41.kA

insulation: ....

Equipment vulnerable to testing: ...DOWNLIGHTS + ALARM.......

RCD tester: ....

Description of Work: ....NEW BUILD................................

Circuit Description	Overcurrent Device * Short-circuit capacity: ...6..kA		Wiring Conductors		Test Results										
					Continuity			Insulation Resistance		Polarity	Earth Loop Imped-ance	Functional Testing		Remarks
	type	Rating I_n	live	cpc	$(R_1 + R_2)$*	R_2*	Ring	Live/ Live	Live/ Earth		Z_s	RCD time	Other	
		A	mm²	mm²	Ω	Ω		MΩ	MΩ		Ω	ms		
1	2	3	4	5	*6	*7	*8	*9	*10	*11	*12	*13	*14	15
1 COOKER	B	32	6·0	2·5	0·21	X	X	>299	>299	✓	0·42	X		OUTLET NOW 2-GANG S/O CUPBOARD
2 POWER UP	B	32	2·5	1·5	0·30	X	✓	>299	>299	✓	0·51	X		INC GARAGE DOOR OPERATOR

Moreover, here is my schedule getting close to completion! I have simply added each recorded R1+R2 to the common Ze and put the relevant figure in the circuit Zs box.

I do hope that you can now see the importance of continuity testing. You should now realise that I have been gently leading you along with the paperwork.
In reality, as soon as you have your R1+R2 figure in the relevant box then you can:

- Tick the polarity confirmed box.
- Do the "add up" of Ze to your R1+R2 and put the result in the Zs box.

Therefore, that is THREE TESTS done at the same time.
Continuity testing IS the cornerstone of testing.

This then makes it even more disturbing to see few electricians doing it properly, or at all. You may be wondering then, "How do they fiddle the sheet without doing the continuity test?" Well that is an easy one. The unscrupulous electrician transposes the equation above into:

R1+R2 = Zs-Ze

You may wonder the reason why I am telling you this? I am assuming that you figure this out yourself and adopt it into your working practice. Do not be tempted. The "fiddle" is forbidden because, as a competent person you:

- Have to prove an earth path before energising. (EEBADS).
- Have to prove correct polarity before energising.

To run "the fiddle" involves energising an *untested circuit* and hoping that you find it is earthed. If you go for membership of a self- certification scheme, the inspector will be looking out for it because it is one of the oldest tricks in the book. He will not tolerate this so you have been warned.

At this stage of the job now, you once again need to put your designer's hat on. Looking at the schedule above, we have calculated values of Zs for our two circuits.

We need to check these two measured values against the maximums laid down in the OSG.

You should now be starting to find your way around the OSG, but if not, go once again to the appendices on **p6 OSG**. Here you should spot appendix 2 which is "maximum permissible measured earth loop impedance" This will send you to **p88 OSG**.

Now skip the pages until you come to the page concerning mcbs. It is on **p92 OSG**.

Our cooker and upstairs ring are both protected by B32 A mcbs. The table displays:

- Maximum Zs for a B32 mcb is 1.20Ω.

Referring to the above schedule of results, our measured maximum earth loop impedances for the circuits are:

- Cooker 0.42Ω.
- Upstairs ring 0.51Ω.

You can see then that these circuits pass. In layman's terms:

- Our measured figures are lower than the allowed maximum.
- In the event of an earth fault, more than enough current will flow in line with Ohm's Law.
- The breaker will trip out well within the maximum disconnection time.
- The house will not burn down or no one should be electrocuted!

If you go back to look at the design part of this book, you will remember that, in theory, as long as we keep a circuit within a set length then it cannot fail to work properly. This is still a fact but the regulations still require you to record the actual earth loop impedance and check it against the maximum listed.

Another thing to mention now is the maximum Zs figures themselves.
Some of the more eagle eyed among you may have spotted that the maximum Zs figures in the OSG are different to those found in BS 7671. As an example I will use the B32 mcb that feeds the circuits we have tested above. The figures given in both books are:

- **Table 2D p92 OSG**   1.20Ω.
- **Table 41B2 p46 BS7671**   1.50Ω.

This is nothing to worry about. I am only showing you this for information only:

- All the maximum Zs figures within the OSG are 80% of those from BS7671.
- As a Part P electrician, the OSG figures are the ones you must use.
- Furthermore, your maximum circuit cable lengths in **Section 7 OSG** are engineered from these 80% OSG values.

The reason for these different figures is not beyond the layman. When a copper conductor heats up its resistance also increases. The maximum Zs figures in BS 7671 are given at a cables maximum operating temperature, which in the case of pvc insulated cable is 70°C. The maximum Zs figures within the OSG are calculated at 10°C - 20°C. Therefore the theory goes that as long as you stay within the OSG figures, then no matter how hot the circuit runs, the real maximum Zs in BS 7671 can never be exceeded. As I said, this discussion is only for your information so for the Part P domestic installer can be disregarded. However, knowledge of it may impress your inspector at scheme membership inspection time!

To finish this section, we now need to go back to our schedule of circuit results. You will notice that on the schedule above one last box needs filling. It is titled "Functional testing, other". This merely means, "Does equipment work properly?"

To complete my testing then:

- I turned on.
- Did a quick live polarity check on my circuits to double check all was well.
- Plugged in the cooker and made sure it turned on and off.
- Ticked the "Functional testing, other" box!

Form 4

SCHEDULE OF TEST RESULTS

Form No   /4

Contractor: MSP
Test Date: 8/5/06
Signature: Alen Lyle
Method of protection against indirect contact: EEBADS
Equipment vulnerable to testing: DOWNLIGHTS + ALARM

Address/Location of distribution board: GARAGE

* Type of Supply: TN-S/TN-C-S/TT
* Ze at origin: 0.21 ohms
* PFC: 1.41 kA

Instruments
loop impedance:
continuity:
insulation:
RCD tester:

Description of Work: NEW BUILD

Circuit Description	Overcurrent Device * Short-circuit capacity: ...6..kA		Wiring Conductors		Test Results										
					Continuity			Insulation Resistance		Polarity	Earth Loop Imped-ance	Functional Testing		Remarks	
	type	Rating I_n	live	cpc	$(R_1 + R_2)*$	R_2*	R i n g	Live/Live	Live/Earth		Z_s	RCD time	Other		
		A	mm²	mm²	Ω *6	Ω *7	*8	MΩ *9	MΩ *10	*11	Ω *12	ms *13	*14		15
1 COOKER	B	32	6·0	2·5	0·21	✗	✗	>299	>299	✓	0·42	✗	✓	OUTLET NOW 2-GANG S/O CUPBOARD
2 POWER UP	B	32	2·5	1·5	0·30	✗	✓	>299	>299	✓	0·51	✗	✓	INC GARAGE DOOR OPERATOR

This is the finished article. All I have to do now is get the rest of it done!

RCD testing P81 OSG

Mains live test	Incoming polarity test
Mains live test	Prospective fault current test
Mains live test	Ext. earth loop impedance test (Ze) or eath electrode test (Ra)
Circuit dead test	Continuity of protective conductors or ring circuit test
Circuit dead test	Insulation resistance test
Circuit dead test	Circuit polarity test
Circuit connected live test	Earth loop impedance test (Zs)
Circuit connected live test	RCD trip time test

As far as our project cooker and upstairs ring goes, that is the testing finished. However, some of our project's circuits are protected by an rcd, which also needs testing.

Before we do that I need to give you a little background information on these devices. Many years ago before they were known as an rcd they were called:

- Earth leakage circuit breakers.

This name, I thought, always described them more sensibly. The device monitors circuit current and trips if it "sees" a certain amount leaking away to earth.

The modern name has been shortened from "residual current device" and that also describes how it works. The unit:

- Monitors current flowing through it on the "live" side and the returning "neutral" side.
- In a healthy circuit, these two currents are equal and the device remains stable.
- If a leakage to earth now occurs, the device "sees" this residue of current escaping and disconnects the circuit.

If a circuit has an RCD fitted, then the RCD test is the last test performed. It has to be last test as you test it by injecting a current down the earth. Therefore, you must prove that an earth exists before you start sending test currents down it. If there was no earth then you could give someone, somewhere on the installation a nasty shock!

To summarise then, the purpose of this test is:

- To confirm that, if fitted, an RCD disconnects a circuit during an earth fault within the maximum time laid down in the regulations.

P81 OSG explains all this in detail but I shall read between the lines to simplify things. The first thing to note is that there are two types of RCD. The powers that be, who by experiment have decided in years gone by, that the maximum safe shock current that a man can survive is around 50mA. Notice now this is a small "m" This means milliamps or thousandths of an amp.

Obviously then the current limit on an RCD is set to a more conservative figure of 30mA. This is the reason why when you purchase a "split-load" type consumer unit it always has a 30mA RCD fitted.

It is possible to buy an rcd with a trip current greater than 30mA so you may say "What is the point of fitting one if it won't save me from electrocution?" This leads us nicely to the definitions of both types of rcd:

- Any RCD up to and including 30mA is for direct contact or shock protection.
- Any RCD above 30mA is for indirect contact or fire protection only.

If you take another look at the left hand column of the schedule of inspections on **p131 OSG**, you will see two rcd boxes. One is for direct contact protection. The other one is for indirect contact protection. If you fit a 30mA or less rcd then you can tick both boxes. If you were to fit an rcd larger than 30mA for whatever reason, then you would only tick the "indirect contact" rcd box. The "direct contact" box would be marked n/a.

Before I demonstrate rcd testing on our project we need to discuss where we **must** fit an rcd. The four main ones you will come across are:

Sockets that may reasonably be used to supply equipment for use outdoors.

Even though EEBADS is good, it is by no means perfect. If you somehow made direct contact with say a frayed flex while stood in the garden you could receive a shock of perhaps 200mA. If this was to happen, then you would be killed as the mcb or fuse protecting this circuit could be of 20 or 32A rating. As you know you need a large fault current to disconnect a circuit, and the protective device would not "see" 1/5 of an amp flowing through you! If a 30mA rcd is fitted then you will be saved as it can "see" this leakage current. The need for this 30mA rcd is demonstrated in my diagram on **p26**.

T-T installations.

In this sort of installation, you can never have huge fault currents flowing during earth faults. This is because the earth itself is not a very good conductor of electricity. As an example, lets say you have an immersion heater protected by a B16 mcb and a Zs figure of 40Ω. (this is quite a good figure for a T-T!). **P92 OSG** tells us the maximum Zs for this circuit is 2.40Ω. Now going back to Ohms law at the beginning of this book, it shows that if an earth fault were to occur on this circuit then the maximum fault current that could flow would be:

$$I= V/Z$$
$$I= 240/40$$
$$I= 6A!$$

Therefore, you can see that the mcb will never trip and the house could burn down! Referring to what I have already showed you then a 100 or even a 500mA fire protection RCD will do the job perfectly. This bigger RCD is usually used as a main switch for the whole installation. It could also be an "S type" time delay unit. This is illustrated on **p21-22 OSG**. The reason for a time delayed main RCD is that if a fault occurs on a socket circuit, then the whole house should not be plunged into darkness. On a T-T installation, any sockets which could be used to supply portable equipment outdoors, have to be on a 30mA rcd, no matter what rcd is fitted elsewhere within the installation.

Circuits with an excessive Zs

This is basically the same as the T-T scenario. If the measured Zs is higher than that allowed then th quick fix is to rcd protect it.

Rooms containing a bath or shower, other than bathrooms

Look at **p60 OSG** for guidance on this point. The main one here is where say a bedroom contains a wal in shower or bath. The sockets must be outside zone 3 and 30mA rcd protected.

The text regarding the tests within the regulations on OSG is a little difficult to follow so I will re produce the tests exactly as I show my students in class.

Up to and including 30m A	Above 30m A
Shock potection & Direct contact	Fire protection & Indirect contact only
1/2 X I test (no trip)	1/2 X I test (no trip)
1 X I test (200mS max)	1 X I test (200mS max)
5X I test (40mS max)	**5X I test (NO TEST)**
"T" test Button	"T" test Button

The "I" shown here is the actual trip current of the rcd.

Therefore, a 30mA rcd has the tests done at:

- 15, 30 and 150mA (that's 1/2, 1 and 5 times).
  A 20mA trip would be tested at 10, 20, 100mA, and so on.

- Note that a fire or indirect contact protection rcd is not subjected to the five times test.

Before I demonstrate there are just a few more things to discuss. Our European neighbours test rcc differently from us. You may see on your tester a "ramp testing" setting and a switch for 0° and 180° Read your tester's instructions and have a play with it by all means but do not worry about any of i Leave your machine on its default setting and do the tests as shown. The default setting is usually 0° In addition, the OSG tells us that the maximum trip time for a BS type rcd is 200mS. It then goes on t state that a BSEN type has a maximum trip time of 300mS. If we disregard this and stick to a universa 200mS limit we will be erring on the side of safety and have less to remember!

I have found a convenient socket, which is rcd protected, and set the tester on it's 30mA setting. I have also now set it to the 1/2 current test and pressed the button. The trip time shown here is "greater than 1999mS", which is greater than 2 seconds. This means the unit did not trip and has passed! The first rcd test is complete.

I have now put the tester on its one times current test, pressed the button and tripped the rcd in 37mS. The table on the previous page declares a maximum trip time of 200mS so this has passed it's next test.

Now I have reset the rcd and switched my test instrument to its five times current test. I have again pressed the button and tripped the unit. It tripped in 12mS. Once again checking the table it has to trip within 40mS so is declared a "pass".

The very last test now is a functional check. I simply press the test or "T" button and the unit should trip out. I then reset it and the testing is complete.

This picture is of the finished consumer unit. It is a split-load type unit. The main switch is on the far right. Next to this switch, you will spot a number of mcbs. These are not rcd protected. To the left of the bank of mcbs you can see the rcd with its yellow test button. The three mcbs to the left of the rcd are protected by the rcd. The silver label at the top of the unit is the rcd information sticker. To comply with BS7671, you must not forget to fit it. The wording of this label is reproduced on **p39 OSG**.

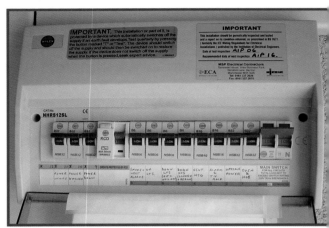

SCHEDULE OF TEST RESULTS

Contractor: _MSP_
Test Date: _8/5/06_
Signature _Alan Lynn_
Method of protection against indirect contact: _EEBADS_
Equipment vulnerable to testing: _DOWNLIGHTS + ALARM_

Address/Location of distribution board: _GARAGE_

* Type of Supply: TN-S/TN-C-S/TT
* Ze at origin: _0.21_ ohms
* PFC: _1.41_ kA

Instruments
loop impedance: _____
continuity: _____
insulation: _____
RCD tester: _____

Description of Work: _NEW BUILD_

Circuit Description	Overcurrent Device *Short-circuit capacity: _6_ kA		Wiring Conductors		Continuity			Insulation Resistance		P o l a r i t y	Earth Loop Imped-ance	Functional Testing		Remarks
	type	Rating In	live	cpc	(R₁+R₂)*	R₂*	Ring	Live/Live	Live/Earth		Zs	RCD time	Other	
		A	mm²	mm²	Ω	Ω		MΩ	MΩ		Ω	ms		
1	2	3	4	5	*6	*7	*8	*9	*10	*11	*12	*13	*14	15
1 COOKER	B	32	6.0	2.5	0.21	X	X	>299	>299	✓	0.42	X	✓	OUTLET NOW 2-GANG S/O CUPBOARD
2 POWER UP.	B	32	2.5	1.5	0.30	X	✓	>299	>299	✓	0.51	X	✓	INC. GARAGE DOOR OPERATOR
3 ALARM + TV	B	16	2.5	1.5	0.04	X	X	>299	>299	✓	0.25	X	✓	FITTED IN GARAGE
4 CENT. HTG	B	10	1.5	1.0	0.29	X	X	>299	>299	✓	0.50	X	✓	BOILER IN GARAGE
5 LTG. DOWN	B	6	1.5	1.0	1.26	X	X	>299	>299	✓	1.47	X	✓	LOUNGE, HALL + BED ECT.
6 LTG. DOWN	B	6	1.5	1.0	1.00	X	X	>299	>299	✓	1.21	X	✓	KITCHEN, UTILITY + BELL CCT.
7 LTG. UP.	B	6	1.5	1.0	1.18	X	X	>299	>299	✓	1.39	X	✓	
8 SMOKES + HEAT	B	6	1.5	1.0	0.93	X	X	>299	>299	✓	1.14	X	✓	
9 POWER DOWN	B	32	2.5	1.5	0.73	X	✓	>299	165	✓	0.94	37	✓	
10 POWER KIT	B	32	2.5	1.5	0.36	X	✓	>299	>299	✓	0.57	37	✓	
11 POWER UTILITY	B	32	2.5	1.5	0.17	X	✓	>299	>299	✓	0.38	37	✓	+ 2 GANG S/O ADJ TO MAINS IN GARAGE

└→ 5x TRIP TIME 12mS.

Deviations from Wiring Regulations and special notes:

* See notes on schedule of test results

Page 4 of 4

Here is the finished schedule. The three circuits on the RCD-protected side of the consumer unit are circuits:

- 9   Downstairs power.
- 10 Kitchen power.
- 11 Utility power.

The first thing to note is that I did not test each circuit. They are all connected to a common rcd so my trip time results can be triplicated.

The figures are entered as follows:

- Half times current test.   This is not entered anywhere.
- One times current test.   This figure goes into column 13.
- Five times current test.   This figure has nowhere to go. I have put it in the notes box.

Before I move onto the next section I would like to deal with a couple of rcd myths that are mentioned quite regularly among the electrical community.

MYTH   *Rcds sometimes suffer from "mystery tripping". That's just the way it is.*

This is definitely not true. The only thing that can trip an RCD is a fault. It will either be an appliance that is plugged in or the installation is faulty. We are concerned with electrical installation so I will deal with that. If an installation is suffering with intermittent tripping it can be only one thing. This is the dreaded neutral to earth insulation fault that was discussed in the insulation resistance testing section. Please look at the following diagram.

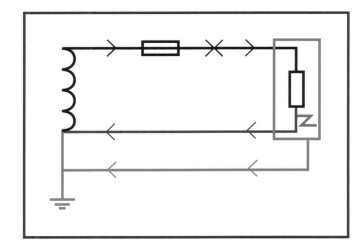

The circuit above has a neutral to earth fault present. The current arrives from the live side of the supply and goes into the load. On the return side the current then splits. Most of the return current goes down the neutral and a little bit runs down the earth. These currents will be in proportion to the resistances of the neutral and earth in line with ohms law. The proportion will always remain the same. So then to explain with examples.

The rcd on this circuit is a 30mA trip and 0.002% of the return current is leaking down the circuit cpc:

- Plug in a load of 1A and 2mA leaks to earth. No trip.
- Plug in a load of 10A and 20mA leaks to earth. Still no trip.
- Plug in a 2kW kettle as well, now the load goes up to 18A. Now 36mA leaks and TRIP!

Of course you will never have this problem, as you will test your work properly and only know of it, not experience it!

This is a scary one which I have heard a few times. If an electrician fits a nice new metal consumer un
on a T-T install, he will naturally need an rcd as a main switch. In this state all the circuits will be pro
tected. The only problem is that the tails *supplying* the unit will not. As we have seen previously a T-
job could have a Ze of perhaps 40Ω plus. Following ohms law then, if the live tail fell out of the mai
switch and touched the metal unit, then we would have a current flowing to earth of:

- I= V/Z, now putting the figures in,
- I=240/40, so the fault current would be 6A!

So, in this situation we would have a current flowing to earth of 6A trying to rupture a main fuse c
perhaps 100A. This is a serious shock and fire hazard. The rule on a T-T install then is to fit an insulate
unit. If you were to come across one of these jobs on your travels, my advice would be to fit an insula
ed enclosure with an RCD fitted in it. Then simply run the tails supplying the consumer unit *through* i
Of course, it goes without saying that you must contact your local supplier regarding this job in respe
of safe isolation / main fuse removal. We have discussed this in detail on **p50**.

It is inevitable that you are occasionally going to get bad readings from your tests.

The purpose of this part is to:

- Give you advice on what has gone wrong and how to correct it.

There are only two faults that could hamper you on your domestic activities. These are:

- A squashed or nailed wire causing an insulation fault (short circuit).
- A loose or broken wire (open circuit).

There exists a lot of hearsay regarding fault-finding. The primary one is:

MYTH   *Fault-finding is definitely not for anyone except a skilled craftsman.*

This is definitely not true. With a little tuition from me and using a little logical thinking, anyone can successfully locate and remedy a circuit defect.

The short circuit scenario

This is not as hard as you would at first believe. Imagine this scenario:

- You have wired a shower circuit a month ago.
- The builders have been in to finish the bathroom and the rest of the house.
- You arrive to finish the shower installation.
- You perform an insulation resistance test. There is a fault. It is a live-earth dead short.
- You check at the obvious places like the pull switch and shower and everything looks good.

So then, you have either a squashed cable somewhere or perhaps a nail through it. This could be bad news but you are armed with your trusty OSG.

Go to p6 OSG. Here you will see appendix 9.

It is titled "*Resistance of copper and aluminium conductors*".
In this table, the institute have measured the resistance of every permutation of cable and given you a resistance figure in mΩ (milliohms) per metre. It is more commonly known as the R1+R2 table.

Let us now go back to the problem. When you did an insulation resistance test you got a dead short between live and earth of 0.00MΩ. What you need to do now is switch your tester to its low resistance setting to get a more accurate reading. Now when you measure again you get a reading. I will make one up of 0.16Ω. The circuit you wired is in 6mm² twin and earth cable.
You know that a 6mm² twin and earth cable has a 2.5mm² cpc so now you can look at the table.

I-ON

The way to use the table is as follows:

- Use the first column to look up your live or phase conductor size.
- Use the second column to look up your cpc size.
- Read across to the third column to find the R1+R2 in mΩ per metre for that cable.

If you line up the 6mm² in column one with 2.5mm² in column two, you should now be looking a 10.49mΩ in column three. Ignore the fourth column, this is for aluminium conductors.

So now, we have:

- A "fault "on our circuit of 0.16Ω total.
- A reading of 10.49mΩ per metre for this fault.

Here you will see that one figure is in "ohms" and the other is in "milliohms" or thousandths of a ohm. We need to convert one of these figures so they are both in the same units. I, like most peopl hate decimal points so will convert:

- 0.16Ω to 160mΩ. Remember 1ohm = 1,000milliohms.

The maths now is easy, the fault "total" is 160mΩ and the fault comes from a figure of 10.49mΩ pe metre.

All that is left now is to do the sum:

- 160/10.49= 15.2m

The fault is around 15 metres from the mains position!

One thing to mention briefly is that the resistance of copper increases with temperature. The tabl is based on the temperature of 20°C. If you happen to be "fault finding" on a boiling hot day or freezing one, the figures will stray a little. If you want to, and have a thermometer handy there is multiplier table on **p159 OSG** to help you adjust the R1+R2 figure.

The R1+R2 table is a very handy thing to have to hand, but we are adapting it for our own purpose In the design part of this book, you saw how the IEE have given you maximum circuit lengths. This the table they have also used!

The open circuit scenario

This one you may find during R1+R2 testing. If you have an open live or earth on a circuit then you w "lose" your reading somewhere on the circuit while continuity testing. If you have an open neutra however, you will not know anything about it until you switch on. When you do switch on, nothin past the open neutral will work. This will be a simple process of elimination to find the problem. Don forget though, you could have had an insulation fault on the open part of the circuit, when you fix make sure you repeat all the tests.

In part seven we covered the inspection and testing of an installation. The general consensus was that t is the best practice to have a rough schedule of circuit results fixed onto the wall adjacent to the onsumer unit. The procedure then is to test in the correct order and record the results on the schedule s you obtain them. The last job is to dress in and terminate the circuits.

n theory then, as you terminate the last wire, you should be filling in the last boxes.

f you do this on your job, then you could say that you have nearly finished the Electrical Installation Certificate.

n OSG domestic type EIC consists of four pages. This certificate is shown on **p129 OSG**. Ve have already done the toughest pages! They also happen to be pages three and four. herefore, we will cover the certificate in reverse order. Everything is re-produced below.

Form 4
Form No   /4

SCHEDULE OF TEST RESULTS

Contractor: *M S P*   Address/Location of distribution board: Instruments

Test Date: *8/5/06*   *GARAGE*   * Type of Supply: TN-S/TN-C-S/TT   loop impedance:

Signature   * Ze at origin: *0·21* ohms   continuity:

Method of protection against indirect contact: *EEBADS*   * PFC: *1·41* kA   insulation:

Equipment vulnerable to testing: *DOWNLIGHTS + ALARM*   RCD tester:

Description of Work: *NEW BUILD*

Circuit Description	Overcurrent Device * Short-circuit capacity: ..6..kA		Wiring Conductors		Continuity			Insulation Resistance		Polarity	Earth Loop Imped-ance	Functional Testing		Remarks
	type	Rating I_n	live	cpc	$(R_1 + R_2)^*$	R_2^*	Ring	Live/ Live	Live/ Earth		Z_s	RCD time	Other	
		A	mm²	mm²	Ω	Ω		MΩ	MΩ		Ω	ms		
1	2	3	4	5	*6	*7	*8	*9	*10	*11	*12	*13	*14	15
1 COOKER	B	32	6·0	2·5	0·21	X	X	>299	>299	✓	0·42	X	✓	OUTLET NOW 2-GANG S/O CUPBOARD
2 POWER UP.	B	32	2·5	1·5	0·30	X	✓	>299	>299	✓	0·51	X	✓	INC. GARAGE DOOR OPERATOR
3 ALARM + TV	B	16	2·5	1·5	0·04	X	X	>299	>299	✓	0·25	X	✓	FITTED IN GARAGE
4 CENT. HTG	B	10	1·5	1·0	0·29	X	X	>299	>299	✓	0·50	X	✓	BOILER IN GARAGE
5 LTG. DOWN	B	6	1·5	1·0	1·26	X	X	>299	>299	✓	1·47	X	✓	LOUNGE, HALL + BED CCT.
6 LTG. DOWN	B	6	1·5	1·0	1·00	X	X	>299	>299	✓	1·21	X	✓	KITCHEN, UTILITY + BELL CCT.
7 LTG. UP.	B	6	1·5	1·0	1·18	X	X	>299	>299	✓	1·39	X	✓	
8 SMOKES + HEAT	B	6	1·5	1·0	0·93	X	X	>299	>299	✓	1·14	X	✓	
9 POWER DOWN	B	32	2·5	1·5	0·73	X	✓	>299	165	✓	0·94	37	✓	
10 POWER KIT	B	32	2·5	1·5	0·36	X	✓	>299	>299	✓	0·57	37	✓	
11 POWER UTILITY	B	32	2·5	1·5	0·17	X	✓	>299	>299	✓	0·38	37	✓	+ 2 GANG S/O ADJ TO MAINS IN GARAGE

Deviations from Wiring Regulations and special notes:

→ 5x TRIP TIME 12 mS.

* See notes on schedule of test results

Page 4 of 4

---

his one you should be sick of seeing by now. It is the schedule of tests and is "Page four of four". his is marked on the bottom right hand corner of the document.

I-ON

Form 3   Form No   /3
SCHEDULE OF INSPECTIONS

| **Methods of protection against electric shock** | **Prevention of mutual detrimental influence** |

Methods of protection against electric shock

(a) Protection against both direct and indirect contact:

[✓] (i)   SELV (note 1)

[N/A] (ii)   Limitation of discharge of energy

(b) Protection against direct contact: (note 2)

[✓] (i)   Insulation of live parts

[✓] (ii)   Barriers or enclosures

[N/A] (iii) Obstacles (note 3)

[N/A] (iv) Placing out of reach (note 4)

[N/A] (v)   PELV

[✓] (vi) Presence of RCD for supplementary protection

(c) Protection against indirect contact:

(i)   EEBADS including:

[✓]   Presence of earthing conductor

[✓]   Presence of circuit protective conductors

[✓]   Presence of main equipotential bonding conductors

[N/A]   Presence of supplementary equipotential bonding conductors

[N/A]   Presence of earthing arrangements for combined protective and functional purposes

[N/A]   Presence of adequate arrangements for alternative source(s), where applicable

[✓]   Presence of residual current device(s)

[✓] (ii)   Use of Class II equipment or equivalent insulation (note 5)

[N/A] (iii) Non-conducting location: (note 6) Absence of protective conductors

[N/A] (iv) Earth-free equipotential bonding: (note 7) Presence of earth-free equipotential bonding conductors

[N/A] (v)   Electrical separation (note 8)

Inspected by .....A. LYNCH.............................

Prevention of mutual detrimental influence

[✓] (a)   Proximity of non-electrical services and other influences

[✓] (b)   Segregation of band I and band II circuits or band II insulation used

[N/A] (c)   Segregation of safety circuits

Identification

[✓] (a)   Presence of diagrams, instructions, circuit charts and similar information

[✓] (b)   Presence of danger notices and other warning notices

[✓] (c)   Labelling of protective devices, switches and terminals

[✓] (d)   Identification of conductors

Cables and conductors

[✓] (a)   Routing of cables in prescribed zones or within mechanical protection

[✓] (b)   Connection of conductors

[✓] (c)   Erection methods

[✓] (d)   Selection of conductors for current-carrying capacity and voltage drop

[✓] (e)   Presence of fire barriers, suitable seals and protection against thermal effects

General

[✓] (a)   Presence and correct location of appropriate devices for isolation and switching

[✓] (b)   Adequacy of access to switchgear and other equipment

[✓] (c)   Particular protective measures for special installations and locations

[✓] (d)   Connection of single-pole devices for protection or switching in phase conductors only

[✓] (e)   Correct connection of accessories and equipment

[N/A] (f)   Presence of undervoltage protective devices

[✓] (g)   Choice and setting of protective and monitoring devices for protection against indirect contact and/or overcurrent

[✓] (h)   Selection of equipment and protective measures appropriate to external influences

[✓] (i)   Selection of appropriate functional switching devices

Date ....8/5/06................

Notes:

✓   to indicate an inspection has been carried out and the result is satisfactory
X   to indicate an inspection has been carried out and the result was unsatisfactory
N/A   to indicate the inspection is not applicable
LIM   to indicate that, exceptionally, a limitation agreed with the person ordering the work prevented the inspection or test being carried out

1.   SELV An extra-low voltage system which is electrically separated from Earth and from other systems. The particular requirements of the Regulations must be checked (see Regulations 411-02 and 471-02)

2.   Method of protection against direct contact - will include measurement of distances where appropriate

3.   Obstacles - only adopted in special circumstances (see Regulations 412-04 and 471-06)

4.   Placing out of reach - only adopted in special circumstances (see Regulations 412-05 and 471-07)

5.   Use of Class II equipment - infrequently adopted and only when the installation is to be supervised (see Regulations 413-03 and 471-09)

6.   Non-conducting locations - not applicable in domestic premises and requiring special precautions (see Regulations 413-04 and 471-10)

7.   Earth-free local equipotential bonding - not applicable in domestic premises, only used in special circumstances (see Regulations 413-05 and 471-11)

8.   Electrical separation (see Regulations 413-06 and 471-12)

You should also remember this one. It is the third page and is schedule of inspections that you complete in Part 7. Note this one is marked "Page 3 of 4"

PARTICULARS OF INSTALLATION REFERRED TO IN THE CERTIFICATE Tick boxes and enter details, as appropriate

Means of Earthing

Distributor's facility ☑

Maximum Demand

Maximum demand (load)........ *65* .... Amps per phase

Details of Installation Earth Electrode (*where applicable*)

Installation earth electrode ☐

Type (e.g. rod(s), tape etc)	Location	Electrode resistance to earth
	N/A	.... Ω

Main Protective Conductors

Earthing conductor: material ..... *C U* ..... csa ..... *16* .....mm² connection verified ☑

Main equipotential bonding conductors material ..... *C U* ..... csa ..... *10* .....mm² connection verified ☑

To incoming water and/or gas service ☑ To other elements .... *NONE* .

Main Switch or Circuit-breaker

BS, Type ..*60947*.... No. of poles ...*2*... Current rating *100* A Voltage rating *240* V

Location *FITTED IN CON UNIT* Fuse rating or setting ..*N/A* A

Rated residual operating current $I_{\Delta n}$ = *N/A* mA, and operating time of *N/A* ms (at $I_{\Delta n}$) (applicable only where an RCD is suitable and is used as a main circuit-breaker)

COMMENTS ON EXISTING INSTALLATION: (In the case of an alteration or additions see Section 743)

....

.... *NONE* ....

....

....

....

....

SCHEDULES (note 2)

The attached Schedules are part of this document and this Certificate is valid only when they are attached to it.

....*1*.... Schedules of Inspections and ....*1*.... Schedules of Test Results are attached.

(Enter quantities of schedules attached).

GUIDANCE FOR RECIPIENTS

This safety Certificate has been issued to confirm that the electrical installation work to which it relates has been designed, constructed and inspected and tested in accordance with British Standard 7671 (The IEE Wiring Regulations).

You should have received an original Certificate and the contractor should have retained a duplicate Certificate. If you were the person ordering the work, but not the user of the installation, you should pass this Certificate, or a full copy of it including the schedules, immediately to the user.

The "original" Certificate should be retained in a safe place and be shown to any person inspecting or undertaking further work on the electrical installation in the future. If you later vacate the property, this Certificate will demonstrate to the new owner that the electrical installation complied with the requirements of British Standard 7671 at the time the Certificate was issued. The Construction (Design and Management) Regulations require that for a project covered by those Regulations, a copy of this Certificate, together with schedules is included in the project health and safety documentation.

For safety reasons, the electrical installation will need to be inspected at appropriate intervals by a competent person. The maximum time interval recommended before the next inspection is stated on Page 1 under "Next Inspection".

This Certificate is intended to be issued only for a new electrical installation or for new work associated with an alteration or addition to an existing installation. It should not have been issued for the inspection of an existing electrical installation. A "Periodic Inspection Report" should be issued for such a periodic inspection.

Page 2 of *4* (note 5)

This is a new page for you to look at. It is page two of the project EIC. You will notice that there is not much to write. However there are a few things, which need looking at. Probably now though, you could fill out most of this without instruction. All the relevant information boxes are described below.

Means of Earthing

Distributor's facility ☑

Installation earth electrode ☐

Ours is a TN-C-S supply so I have ticked "Distributor's facility"

Maximum Demand

Maximum demand (load)............. 65 .... Amps per phase

For the vast majority of domestic jobs this box has no relevance. The official line is to have a look a the installation, and using **p84-87 OSG** make an estimate of the maximum demand. In reality, you do what electricians term a "guessomatic" and put a figure in. It must also be stated that domestic installer scheme providers DO NOT like you to enter the value of the main fuse though in reality this the maximum demand.

Details of Installation Earth Electrode (*where applicable*)

Type	Location	Electrode resistance to earth
(e.g. rod(s), tape etc)	N/A	
		.... Ω

If you had ticked "installation earth electrode" in the box at the top of this page, this is where you would put the electrode details. I have given this box a big N/A, as there is no electrode.

Main Protective Conductors

Earthing conductor: material .... C u .... csa .... 16 ....mm²   connection verified ☑

Main equipotential bonding conductors   material .... C u .... csa .... 10 ....mm²   connection verified ☑

To incoming water and/or gas service ☑   To other elements .... NONE . ....

This is the box where you record the arrangement of the main protective conductors. It is self-explanatory. All sizes are shown on **p27-29 OSG**

Main Switch or Circuit-breaker

BS, Type ..60947....   No. of poles ...2....   Current rating 100...A   Voltage rating ..240..V

Location FITTED IN CON UNIT   Fuse rating or setting .N/A.A

Rated residual operating current I_Δn = .N/A. mA, and operating time of .N/A.ms (at I_Δn) (applicable only where an RCD is suitable and is used as a main circuit-breaker)

This is a nice easy box! You simply read exactly what it says on the main switch. You then record it here. Note that I have not mentioned the rcd of our split-load consumer unit. This is because our rcd is *not* the main switch. On a T-T system with a main switch rcd, you would record the details of it here Also, note the N/A in the "fuse rating or setting" part of this box. Our main switch does not have any over-current protection, it is merely an on/off switch.

COMMENTS ON EXISTING INSTALLATION: (In the case of an alteration or additions see Section 743)

....
.... *NONE* ....
....
....
....
....
....
....

In this box, I have stated "none". It is a new job so there are no comments. If you are doing one or two new circuits in a house, this is where you would put any comments. You could comment on:

- Damaged accessories.
- No existing certificate or circuit chart.
- The need for a periodic inspection.

SCHEDULES (note 2)
The attached Schedules are part of this document and this Certificate is valid only when they are attached to it.
.....1..... Schedules of Inspections and .....1..... Schedules of Test Results are attached.
(Enter quantities of schedules attached).

The last thing to look at on page two is this box. Our EIC has one inspection schedule and one test results schedule. You must state what the certificate is made up of.

That takes care of "Page two of four", so now we shall take a look at page one.

Form 1

Form No   /1

ELECTRICAL INSTALLATION CERTIFICATE (notes 1 and 2)
(REQUIREMENTS FOR ELECTRICAL INSTALLATIONS - BS 7671 [IEE WIRING REGULATIONS])

DETAILS OF THE CLIENT (note 1)
XYZ CONTRACTING LTD,
HOWMUCH HOUSE,
CHADDERTON OLDHAM.

INSTALLATION ADDRESS
19 VICTORIA WAY
BRAMHALL STOCKPORT
Postcode *SK7 1DR*

DESCRIPTION AND EXTENT OF THE INSTALLATION Tick boxes as appropriate

Description of installation: *NEW BUILD.*

New installation	☑

Extent of installation covered by this Certificate: ....
ALL OF IT.

Addition to an existing installation	☐
Alteration to an existing installation	☐

FOR DESIGN, CONSTRUCTION, INSPECTION & TESTING
I being the person responsible for the Design, Construction, Inspection & Testing of the electrical installation (as indicated by my signature below), particulars of which are described above, having exercised reasonable skill and care when carrying out the Design, Construction, Inspection & Testing, hereby CERTIFY that the said work for which I have been responsible is to the best of my knowledge and belief in accordance with BS 7671 *2001* amended to *2004* (date) except for the departures, if any, detailed as follows:

Details of departures from BS 7671 (Regulations 120-01-03, 120-02):

NONE.

The extent of liability of the signatory is limited to the work described above as the subject of this Certificate.

Name (IN BLOCK LETTERS): *ALAN LYNCH*   Position: *ELECTRICIAN.*
Signature (note 3): ....   Date: *10/05/06*
For and on behalf of: *MSP CONTRACTING LTD.*
Address: *DOWNSIDE HOUSE, TAME BUSINESS*
PARK DENTON   Postcode *M34 0VS*   Tel No: *123 4567*

NEXT INSPECTION
I recommend that this installation is further inspected and tested after an interval of not more than *10* years/months (notes 4 and 7)

SUPPLY CHARACTERISTICS AND EARTHING ARRANGEMENTS Tick boxes and enter details, as appropriate

Earthing arrangements	Number and Type of Live Conductors	Nature of Supply Parameters	Supply Protective Device Characteristics
TN-C ☐	a.c. ☑ d.c. ☐	Nominal voltage, U/U₀$^{(1)}$ *230* V	Type: *BS 1361*
TN-S ☐	1-phase, 2-wire ☑ 2-pole ☐	Nominal frequency, f $^{(1)}$ *50* Hz	Nominal current rating *100* A
TN-C-S ☑	1-phase, 3-wire ☐ 3-pole ☐	Prospective fault current, I_pf $^{(2)}$ *1·41* kA (note 6)	
TT ☐	2-phase, 3-wire ☐ other ☐		
IT ☐	3-phase, 3-wire ☐	External loop impedance, Z_e $^{(2)}$ *0·21* Ω	
Alternative source ☐ of supply (to be detailed on attached schedules)	3-phase, 4-wire ☐	(Note: (1) by enquiry, (2) by enquiry or by measurement)	

Page 1 of *4* (note 5)

The top of page one states:

- The client, that is who is paying for the job.
- Where the job has happened.

This is self-explanatory and I shall not cover it further. Now we shall look at the rest.

DESCRIPTION AND EXTENT OF THE INSTALLATION Tick boxes as appropriate

Description of installation: *NEW BUILD.*

Extent of installation covered by this Certificate: .... *ALL OF IT.*	New installation	☑
	Addition to an existing installation	☐
	Alteration to an existing installation	☐

This first box is a statement of what has been done. You must record exactly what you do so you do not become liable in the future for something you didn't do! As an example, on a job, do not say downstairs sockets, state:

- *"Four two gang sockets and spur for fan light in new conservatory"*

In the box to the right, you tick to indicate what you have generally done:

- New.   Full rewire.
- Addition.   Perhaps a conservatory installation or new shower.
- Alteration.   This is where you convert say an old immersion heater circuit into a socket.

- *Remember, you only issue an EIC for a rewire or new circuit. If you extend an existing circuit, then that is a minor works certificate. This is covered in a following part.*

FOR DESIGN, CONSTRUCTION, INSPECTION & TESTING

I being the person responsible for the Design, Construction, Inspection & Testing of the electrical installation (as indicated by my signature below), particulars of which are described above, having exercised reasonable skill and care when carrying out the Design, Construction, Inspection & Testing, hereby CERTIFY that the said work for which I have been responsible is to the best of my knowledge and belief in accordance with BS 7671 *2001* amended to *2004* (date) except for the departures, if any, detailed as follows:

> Details of departures from BS 7671 (Regulations 120-01-03, 120-02):
>
> *NONE.*

The extent of liability of the signatory is limited to the work described above as the subject of this Certificate.

Name (IN BLOCK LETTERS): *ALAN LYNCH*   Position: *ELECTRICIAN.*
Signature (note 3): ....   Date: *10/05/06*
For and on behalf of: *MSP CONTRACTING LTD.*
Address: *DOWNSIDE HOUSE, TAME BUSINESS PARK DENTON* .... Postcode *M34 0VS.*   Tel No: *123 4567.*

This is the one where you sign your life away! It is pretty straightforward but there are a couple of points to make.

On my job, there were no deviations. If you have any, then this is where you would mention it. A deviation means it is still safe enough, but is not quite compliant with BS 7671. There is not many instances where this would arise but for a couple of examples:

- You wire a new circuit to an existing BS3871 mcb. This is an old type mcb, which is not mentioned in BS7671 any more. It is in the OSG so you can still design a circuit to work on it. Because it is not recognised in BS7671, it can be used but has to be listed as a deviation.

- You rewire a house and cannot get a main equipotential bonding cable to the stop tap in a newly, fully tiled kitchen. If you earth to the mains water in say a cylinder cupboard, it is a deviation.

- For some reason, you cannot reasonably keep a hidden cable within a "safe zone". This is a deviation and would have to be mentioned.

When you fill one of these, do not forget to fill in the dates on the declaration. You have to state which version of the regulations you have done the work to.
The current version is titled BS7671: 2001 (2004)

NEXT INSPECTION

I recommend that this installation is further inspected and tested after an interval of not more than ......*10*...... years/months (notes 4 and 7)

This is where you state the interval of the next inspection. The usual for a domestic is every 10 years, but it is entirely up to you. If the house has ten children thundering up and down the hall on skateboards and you see a cracked switch and socket then recommend 1 year if you like. You cannot be wrong, as it is your opinion only.

Earthing arrangements

TN-C	☐
TN-S	☐
TN-C-S	☑
TT	☐
IT	☐

Alternative source ☒
of supply (to be detailed on attached schedules)

Nice easy one here, you just record the system type of the incoming supply. Also, the installation has no back-up generator (alternative source), so a cross goes in the appropriate box.

Number and Type of Live Conductors

a.c.	☑	d.c.	☐
1-phase, 2-wire	☑	2-pole	☐
1-phase, 3-wire	☐	3-pole	☐
2-phase, 3-wire	☐	other	☐
3-phase, 3-wire	☐		
3-phase, 4-wire	☐		

In this section, you simply tick the correct boxes. The supply into a house is always ac (alternating current) and if single phase always 2-wire. Remember the regulations people class a neutral as a live so the live and neutral coming in to the house are two LIVE conductors.
On 99.9% of domestic installations, this box is always filled the same as this.

Nature of Supply Parameters

Nominal voltage, U/U_0[(1)] ......*230*...... V

Nominal frequency, f[(1)] ......*50*...... Hz

Prospective fault current, I_{pf}[(2)] ......*1.41*...... kA
(note 6)

External loop impedance, Z_e[(2)] ......*0.21*...... Ω

(Note: (1) by enquiry, (2) by enquiry or by measurement)

In this section you have to list the nominal voltage, which is a declared value, not measured, so it is always 230V on a single-phase supply. The next box is the frequency of the supply. It is always 50 Hertz. This means that the alternating current (ticked in the box above) goes backwards and forwards 50 times a second. The last two items which are prospective fault current and external loop impedance, you can lift straight off your draft schedule of test results. YOU measured these, remember?

Supply
Protective Device
Characteristics

Type: _BS 1361_

Nominal current rating
_100_ A

This last box displays the details of the main fuse supplying your installation. As we have discussed previously you are not supposed to go into the supplier's equipment. Usually the details are shown on the side of the main fuse. The BS 1361 is fitted 95% of the time. If for some reason you cannot find out what the fuse is, it is fine and realistic to write unknown.

...nd there it is, all done. I think you can see that 99% of EIC filling will be generic. In other words, once ...ou have done one, you've done them all! The most important thing regarding the form is integrity. ...o not lie or fiddle it, it may come back to haunt you.

...o keep this book to a reasonable size I have not covered the scenario of a three-phase supply.
...n twenty-five years of domestic work, I have only come across two three-phase supplied houses. ...herefore, it is not worth losing sleep over. If you do stumble across one simply take advice from a ...olleague, everyone knows an electrician, maybe not a very good one, but an electrician all the same!

... you join a Part-P self-certification scheme, you will have to fill one of their own EIC certificates. Their ...orm will be easier than this as it is "domestic orientated". Whichever one you fill in it will state at the ...ottom somewhere.

Based on the model in appendix 6 of BS7671"

...his is the form that we have just been filling out!

...ow there is only one piece of paper to complete. On the schedule of inspections, which is page three ...f our certificate, there is a section for "identification". In here, you have ticked "presence of circuit ...harts" and we haven't done one yet!

...ly finished circuit chart is reproduced below.

	DESCRIPTION	POINTS SERVED	CABLE TYPE	CABLE SIZE LIVE	CPC	EEBADS	MCB TYPE	RATING A	IR TEST CAUTION	notes
1	COOKER	1	⌐	6.0	2.5	✓	↗	32	✗	FEEDS 2G. SOCKET.
2	UPSTAIRS POWER	10	⌐	2.5	1.5	✓		32	✗	INC. GARAGE DOOR
3	ALARM + TV AMP	2	⌐	2.5	1.5	✓		16	✓	
4	CENTRAL HTG.	1	⌐	1.5	1.0	✓		10	✓	
5	DOWNSTAIRS LTG	24	W	1.5	1.0	✓	B	6	✓	FRONT OF HOUSE
6	DOWNSTAIRS LTG	12	+	1.5	1.0	✓		6	✓	BACK OF HOUSE
7	UPSTAIRS LTG	10	≥	1.5	1.0	✓		6	✓	
8	SMOKE + HEAT DET.	3		1.5	1.0	✓		6	✓	
9	SOCKETS DOWN	15	≥	2.5	1.5	✓		32	✗	
10	SOCKETS KIT	8		2.5	1.5	✓		32	✗	
11	SOCKETS UTIL.	4	⌐	2.5	1.5	✓	↓	32	✗	+ S/O ADJ TO MAINS.
12										

The completed circuit chart is shown here, tucked inside the consumer unit door.
This is the finished job now, note I have also:

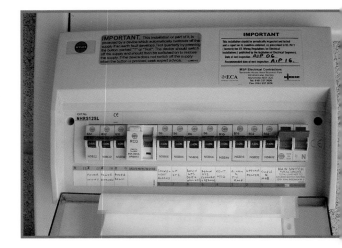

- Marked the breakers up.
- Fitted a 10 year periodic label, that's the yellow one.
- Fitted an rcd label, that's the silver one.

The wording of both labels is shown on
p38 & 39 OSG.

And that is really it now, no catches, honestly. When you break down each operation of installatio the bulk of it really is bordering on common sense. We have now dealt comprehensively with a coupl of myths:

MYTH   *Complying with Part-P is difficult.*
MYTH   *BS7671 paperwork is very difficult.*

Finally, if you do not join a scheme and notify building control of any intended work, they shoul happily accept the paperwork that I have done for you here.
The main thing they are looking for is competence, not a fancy logo on a test sheet.

The Minor Works Certificate or MWC is issued if you do electrical work on a property that does not stretch to the wiring of a new circuit. Examples would include:

- Replacing a broken socket front.
- Replacing a shower unit in a bathroom.
- Fitting wall lights in a lounge, looped off an existing circuit.
- Adding some extra sockets to an existing circuit.

As discussed much earlier, minor works are not notifiable for Part-P unless:

- The minor works occurs in a "special location".

A special location is mainly in regard to bathrooms and kitchens. Remember that a kitchen is not a special location in BS 7671, but is under Part-P.

Please go to **p140-141 OSG** to look at the MWC and accompanying notes.

A minor works is very simple to do and certify. The essential thing to do when looking at a prospective job is to:

- **Preview it properly**.

What I mean to say is, if you went to perform a minor works in the "perfect" world, you would be presented with a "perfect" installation with its correctly filled out EIC and circuit chart. With this rarely found installation, then you could simply add onto the circuit, do a few quick tests and be on your way.

However, in the "real world" you will be confronted with minor works situations on installations that are far from perfect. The work will usually be without a certificate of any kind at best and shoddy at worst. I believe that a domestic installer should have some integrity in his installation work and my solution to this problem is thus. I would either:

- Abandon the minor works and run in a new circuit triggering an EIC or,

- Test the existing circuit to establish if it is of a "minimum" standard to accept your addition and then perform the minor works.

If you opt for the second course of action, I would advise you to perform the following simple tests on the circuit in question before agreeing to do the minor work:

- Do a quick insulation resistance test on the circuit to be added to. Just test between live and neutral to earth. Do not do a live to neutral test, as you will read a short–circuit fault through a TV, video, light fittings etc.

- Do a quick earth loop impedance test (Zs) on the circuit.

I-ON

- In the case of ring circuit extension work, turn off the power and remove a socket close to where you are to perform the minor works. Perform a continuity test on the lives, neutrals and cpc conductors at the socket to make sure there is some sort of ring. The test is the same as the step 1 ring test shown on **p85**. If there is some sort of a ring, you should get a reading between these wires.

If the circuit "passes" these tests, you will be free to proceed. If not then you can either:

- Negotiate the repairs necessary to get the circuit ready for work.
- Price the customer up for a new circuit which will come with an EIC for the new works.

The nightmare scenario is to not preview the job, do the work and then discover the circuit defects afterwards. In effect, you would be responsible for putting the job right at your own cost!
The preview-testing course of action will leave you free from prosecution and a guilty conscience.
I have "walked" from jobs in the past where the customer would not pay for a new circuit and I have not been happy performing a minor works upon it.

It is very rare that I perform minor works, but after I finished the bungalow project, the customer telephoned the office requesting a shaver socket to be fitted in his en-suite bathroom. So, this is how I did it. This is a minor works performed within the "perfect world scenario" that I have described.
In other words, I did not need to preview this job. Lucky me!

The load of a shaver socket is in the order of a negligible 20W so we can add it on to a lighting circuit.

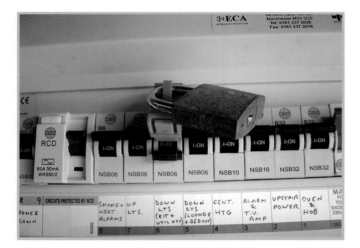

Firstly, I performed a safe isolation and padlocked off the mcb feeding the circuit to be worked on. It is important to lock off now, as there are plenty of unskilled people around the house now! These mcb locks are available at any reputable wholesalers.

You may remember from the insulation testing section that you should test for correct electrical separation on a shaver socket. Here I have the new shaving transformer out of the box. I have set my tester to its 500V insulation test setting. I have the:

- Red probe in the separated output side.
- Black probe in the mains input side at the back of the socket.

The reading of >299MΩ shows that there is no chance of "leakage" from the mains side to the output terminals of the shaver socket.

The shaver socket is to be looped off the lighting circuit as this is the only way to do the job without wrecking the customer's brand new house. I have wired it and I am ready to start testing it.

Following the practice when doing mains circuit testing I have twisted the live and cpc conductors at the light fitting prior to connecting in to this existing lighting joint box.
Then just as an R1+R2 test, I then took a reading between live and earth at the shaver socket input terminal.

I got a reading of 0.04Ω, which is obviously very low.

On the IEE minor works certificate there is only a tick box for this and nowhere to write in any figure.

The box says, "Earth continuity" within the Essential tests section. I can now tick it.

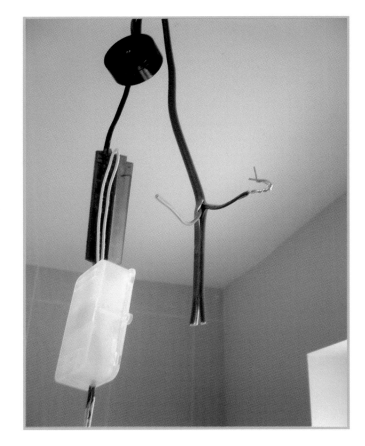

The next job is to perform an insulation resistance test on the new circuit wiring. This is done wit
the cable still disconnected from the lighting joint box. I put the tester back on to its 500V insulatio
resistance setting and tested the cable.
Remember I can not test between live and neutral because the transformer input winding is connecte
across the supply and would show on the tester as a "short circuit fault".

However, I tested live to earth and then neutral to earth and the circuit was declared fine. Bot
readings were found to be >299MΩ. Looking again at **p73 OSG** it can be seen that our insulatio
resistance readings are way above the allowed minimum.

The next job was to connect in the new wiring at the existing light, re-energise and perform an earth loop impedance test. This reading of 1.55Ω is recorded on the minor works certificate in the appropriate box. We will look at this figure later to check if it complies.

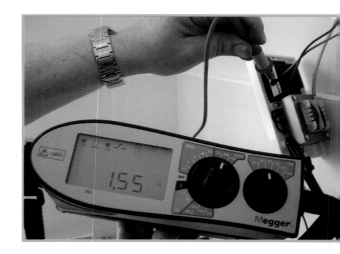

The next job now is to turn off the circuit again and screw back the shaver socket. You can appreciat
that while screwing the shaver socket back I *could* trap a wire in the back of the box and cause a
insulation fault. I therefore like to re-perform the insulation resistance test after screwing back.
could remove the lid from the consumer unit and test there but as you have seen previously ther
are somtimes easier ways to do these jobs! To re-test the insulation resistance I have walked to th
consumer unit and:

- Turned the main switch OFF.
- Turned all the breakers ON.

The next task is to pick a random socket outlet. I have come back to the kitchen as it saves me havin
to bend over! It is a combination of laziness and pending middle-age.

I have re-selected the 500V insulation resistance setting on my tester. Now when I press the button I am checking:

- From the kitchen socket BACK to the consumer unit.

- Through the consumer unit internals.

- And back OUT through ALL the circuits connected to the unit. I am effectively checking the whole house from here, in one operation.

Note that the reading here is now a lot lower than when I checked my small length of un-connected cable before.
This is perfectly normal as I am here testing every wire in the house *and* all the appliances plugged in, at once!
Nevertheless, 83MΩ is still well above the minimums laid down on **p72 OSG**. This installation, with the addition of my new minor works is declared fit for service.

There is just one thing to mention, while discussing this "backwards" insulation testing. If you come across some of these "electronic" rcds or rcbos, you will read a "fault" when IR testing to earth. You will know these devices when you see them. The unit has a little white or cream wire coming from it that is connected to the earth bar. In this case you would have to take the lid off the consumer unit. Then you would have to disconnect the circuit you have just been working on. Finally you would test and re-connect.

Before we look at the certificate, a few more myths for you to peruse:

MYTH *If you do a "little" job for someone, do not bother with paperwork.*
This you do nowadays at your peril. At the time of writing, the Part P prosecutions have begun.

MYTH *If you do a consumer unit change-over, put the work on a MWC.*
I have discussed this before, but it is worth mentioning again. When you change a consumer unit, you change the circuit protection. Therefore, you must design to make sure those new breakers will trip out inside the maximum disconnection times. You must do an EIC for this type of work.

MYTH *If you do a MWC you have to "upgrade" the main bonding to current standards.*
Maybe not. You merely record in the comments section if it is sub-standard. As long as there is some sort of main equipotential bonding present, the job is fine. However, if no main equipotential bonding present, then you must fit it. Remember, you are relying on EEBADS for indirect contact protection.

MYTH *It does not matter if you connect onto a faulty circuit.*

As described above, this is a non-starter. You have an obligation to make sure it is of a reasonable standard, not perfect perhaps, but not lethal either.

MYTH *If you perform minor works on a downstairs socket outlet circuit, and there is no rcd protection, don't worry about it.*

The RCD part of the inspection and testing section, explains why we need an rcd on a socket outlet that could reasonably be likely to supply portable equipment used outdoors. If you work on a downstairs ring or radial circuit, you *must* fit an RCD. Another way to comply would be to fit an RCD socket outlet. Of course the "reasonably likely" bit would mean that you would not have to fit an RCD on an upstairs socket circuit.

On the flip side of all this, if you were to work on an upstairs socket circuit, you would not be required to fit an RCD on the downstairs circuit, as you have not disturbed it. You would be obliged, however, to record this defect in the "comments" part of the MWC.

Form 5

MINOR ELECTRICAL INSTALLATION WORKS CERTIFICATE
(REQUIREMENTS FOR ELECTRICAL INSTALLATIONS - BS 7671 [IEE WIRING REGULATIONS])
To be used only for minor electrical work which does not include the provision of a new circuit

PART 1 : Description of minor works

1. Description of the minor works : *FITTED SHAVER SOCKET (EN-SUITE)*
2. Location/Address : *19 VICTORIA WAY, BRAMMALL, STOCKPORT*
3. Date minor works completed : *28/5/06*
4. Details of departures, if any, from BS 7671

   NONE

PART 2 : Installation details

1. System earthing arrangement: TN-C-S ☑ TN-S ☐ TT ☐
2. Method of protection against indirect contact: *EEBADS*
3. Protective device for the modified circuit : Type BS *60898* Rating *6* A
4. Comments on existing installation, including adequacy of earthing and bonding arrangements : (see Regulation 130-07)

   INSTALLATION OK

PART 3 : Essential Tests

1. Earth continuity : satisfactory ☑
2. Insulation resistance:
   Phase/neutral .... MΩ
   Phase/earth *83* MΩ
   Neutral/earth *83* MΩ
3. Earth fault loop impedance *1·55* Ω
4. Polarity : satisfactory ☑
5. RCD operation (if applicable) : Rated residual operating current I_Δn *N/A* mA and operating time of *N/A* ms (at I_Δn)

PART 4 : Declaration

1. I/We CERTIFY that the said works do not impair the safety of the existing installation, that the said works have been designed, constructed, inspected and tested in accordance with BS 7671 : *2001* (IEE Wiring Regulations), amended to *2004* and that the said works, to the best of my/our knowledge and belief at the time of my/our inspection, complied with BS 7671 except as detailed in Part 1.
2. Name: *ALAN LYNCH*   3. Signature: *Alan Lynch*
   For and on behalf of: *MSP CONTRACTING*   Position: *ELECTRICIAN*
   Address: *DOWNSIDE HOUSE*
   TAME BUSINESS PARK   Date: *28/5/06*
   DENTON

I-ON

This is my minor works certificate for the shaver socket. You can see it is quite straightforward.

There are a few points to make about it though:

- The insulation resistance figures I have recorded are those that I recorded for the whole house after I connected in the shaver socket. You could enter the higher insulation resistance figure I got when I tested my new piece of cable before connection into the lighting joint box. Both figures are above the minimum requirement so either figure will suffice.

- There is no live to neutral insulation reading recorded as the shaver is a fixed load across the supply. In other words, it would show as a wiring "fault". Again, when I performed my "whole house" insulation test, I could not do a live to neutral test. Again, I would read all the appliances plugged as well as the shaver, as a wiring fault.

- The only thing left to check now is the maximum and measured earth loop impedance (Zs) figures for this circuit's protection. **P92 OSG** tells us the maximum Zs for a B6 mcb is 6.40Ω. Our measured value of 1.55Ω is well within the maximum, so the circuit is safe to use.

- The polarity I checked while taking my Zs measurement so could tick that box as correct also.

And that is the MWC taken care of. Just like an EIC, they are usually generic. Once you have done one, you will do any of them literally without a thought.

You can see that minor works involves interfering with an existing circuit and this can cause other issues. To finish this section now I would like to pass on to you a cautionary tale.

A few years ago, a young man took and passed his 2381 (16th Edition) exam. He did his course where I teach now. However, his mother and fiancée came to collect his certificate as he had been electrocuted at work in the meantime. He was a time served electrician, working within good published practice and within the law. So, you may be thinking now, "How can this have happened?"

- He was doing a minor works on a circuit and was killed by a "robbed neutral".

The robbed neutral is a silent killer that lurks within the occasional installation. It is not mentioned much in books, but you need to be aware of the hazard. As usual, it is best illustrated by diagrams.

This drawing shows two normal healthy lighting circuits. The brown and blue lines at the bottom are the connections inside the consumer unit.
The cross symbols on the left are mcbs. As you now know there is nothing wrong with this arrangement.

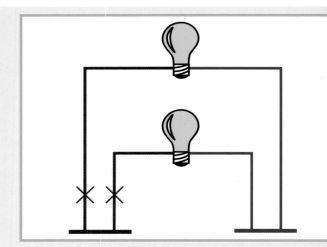

This drawing now shows the robbed neutral in its "hidden" state. The circuits will still function with no apparent problems. Some unscrupulous electrician has added the top light. He has "pinched" a live feed from the consumer unit but then connected the neutral into another circuit.
This will all remain undiscovered until...

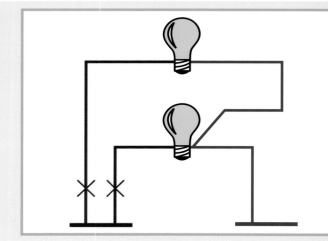

... the unsuspecting electrician comes to work on the bottom light circuit. He will:

- Switch off the mcb as shown.
- Perform a safe isolation.
- Lock off the circuit.
- Begin work.

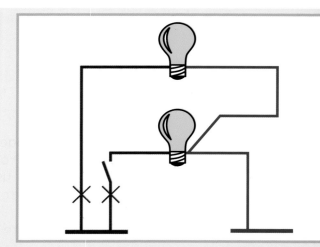

I-ON

136

When he begins work, that is when the hidden killer strikes. The top circuit is still on. As the electrician disconnects the bottom light, he will separate the neutrals. As he does this one of them will become live and he will receive a shock, and as we have seen above perhaps a fatal one. He is effectively connected to the live wire *through* the lamp.

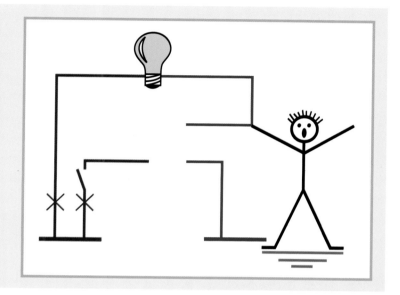

Now before you become worried about this, I have only come across robbed neutrals three times in twenty-five years. It is rare but they are out there.

As a Part-P electrician, you see now that you must always be on your guard when messing with old wiring. I shall now give you the best tips to keep safe in general:

- The safest way is to switch off the whole house, though this is not always possible.

- If you have to leave the installation on, isolate and lock off the circuit as normal.
  When you separate the neutrals, touch them both against a reliable earth.
  If one of them "sparks" then you have found a robbed neutral. Alternatively, you could find the voltage on them with a test lamp or meter. Remember, "robbed neutrals" *can and will* kill.

- Even if no voltage is present, it may become live if something is switched on somewhere else, so do not become complacent.

- If you spend your life "pretending" that everything you work on is live, you won't go far wrong.

- If your job involves crawling around under floors to install wiring, I would advise that you definitely switch off the whole house. You never know what bare live end you may crawl on under that damp floor. And never ever use a mains powered hand lamp. If it goes wrong and you get a shock you will be in big trouble and difficult to rescue.

- Another old sparky routine to finish with now. Even though you will always prove every thing dead... Disconnect in the order live, neutral and earth. Reconnect in the order earth, neutral and live. This is the safest order of work and a good habit to assume, just in case, you see!

Since Part-P has arrived a new myth has surfaced:

MYTH   *The Part- P Scheme membership inspection is like a Spanish inquisition.*

This is definitely not correct. Some people I have spoken to imagine sitting at a desk in a dark room, with a bright light shining in their face! If you go for assessment, then it will be a gentle affair. Your inspector will soon figure out how much you know by chatting with you generally. With the panic over now, please read on for details!

If you have read and digested everything I have told you, and possibly gone on "a five-day wonder" course, then you may be considering membership of one of the government sanctioned schemes. This requires a substantial layout to join, but if you do regular domestic work it will save you a lot of money in the long term. Membership is around £400-£500 per annum(at time of writing), but remember that if you don't run with a scheme then you would be looking at a minimum of around £80 charge per job from building control, no matter how small. In reality then, you have no choice but to join one of the five present schemes.

The way it works is thus. If you are in the scheme you are registered as a "competent person" and do not need to talk to building control. To comply with the law though, building control must be notified. As a member you inform your scheme provider and *they* deal with building control. You simply inform your provider of:

- When you did a job.
- Where you did the job.
- What the job was.

This can be done on line and is usually charged at a couple of pounds per job. They then inform building control to comply with the law and then building control issue a building compliance certificate to the customer to complete the process.

From reports that come through the electrical grapevine, all the present self-certification scheme providers seem to give good service and support, so which one you join will be entirely up to you.

One of the major worries that haunt the potential scheme joiner is rejection of application and this is understandable as a re-visit is usually charged for again. Please do not worry too much about this, as at the end of the day they do want your membership and your money! By bringing you under their wing they are also doing their bit to help improve safety in electrical installation work by guiding you where you may be going wrong slightly. Advice will always be given on how to improve by the inspector.

reality, if you are anyway "on the ball" you will be allowed in. It's a little like when you pass your driving test. The "pass" ticket does not mean you are Michael Schumacher, but merely that you have shown the minimum competence to be allowed out on the road on your own! However they do have bare minimums and certain "major fails" will not be tolerated. If you did the following, these would be the "kiss of death" and rightly so! After reading "The Part P Doctor" you now know how do to do it right, and not like you may have been doing it before!

- Direct contact infringements. For example leaving a live consumer unit with the lid off. Another prime example would be to present a consumer unit with missing breaker "blanks" for your inspection.
- Indirect contact misdemeanours. For example energising a circuit with no main bonding present (EEBADS).
- Energising an untested circuit.
- Having an up and running installation with no certificate present or pending.
- Switching off a main isolator and not then performing a safe isolation check.

Minor mistakes would include for instance:

- No schedule in a consumer unit.
- Breakers or fuses not marked up legibly.
- Wiring not clipped neatly on an installation.

Your provider will warn you in advance as to what documentation you need before a visit but this will include:

- BS7671 and an On-Site Guide.
- A copy of the Electricity at Work act 1989.
- A public liability insurance policy.
- Some sort of health and safety policy.

You can see now that membership is not a big deal, so to speak. It should be obvious that the scheme membership inspection is a lot easier than is commonly perceived. Good luck! I feel sure you won't be needing it!

Well, if you have made it through to here, congratulations. I do hope you have enjoyed reading this as much as I enjoyed writing it. Is "enjoyed" the apt word, I wonder? There is not much more I can tell you now, it is all up to you. Part P compliance can only be gained through experience. If you get "odd" readings on a test, I am not there to help you in person. Do not worry about this, as I get plenty of odd readings also. The secret is to stand back and take stock of the situation. You will eventually see the light, if you excuse my pun! It can be most satisfying to "figure it out" for yourself.

For those who have read and say," Well its easy for him isn't it?" well that is true also, but I had to start somewhere as well. When a young man completes a four-year electrical apprenticeship, he is just as lost as you are going to be, albeit with a background that is a little more technical. As I have said previously this book can be no substitute for proper skills training and experience.

By the way, it does not do any harm to actually read the OSG and BS 7671 now and again. You will find plenty in there that I have not mentioned. For example, when you clip a cable in the loft, how do you know if you are spacing the clips adequately. Well, surprise surprise, the answer is in there somewhere! And don't forget, your scheme inspector will expect to see you becoming more "au fait" with the books and "tech talk" as time rolls by.

A good piece of advice for the Part P rookie is to buy themselves some test equipment and to test their own house. This is an excellent place to get ones teeth into the murky world of test and certification. You should either photocopy the certificates from BS 7671 to practice with or do like me and download them off the internet. To test your house you will need to use a "periodic inspection report" (PIR) form. This is similar to an EIC but includes extra boxes for you to fill. When you do check your house you will be surprised what defects you discover. You could say that taking the time to read this book has opened a Pandora's Box for you! The PIR form is also in the On-site guide.

The last thing to say is that my book cannot cover all eventualities. I have practised as an electrician for a quarter of a century and I haven't seen it all yet. Therefore, if you come across the weird and wonderful such as swimming pools, generating plant or 3-phase supplied houses then you will have to take advice. And you would be surprised where you can get the help you need. How about for starters:

- BS 7671.
- The plant installer.
- The equipment manufacturer.
- If you end up with one, your Part P scheme provider technical help line.
- Local building control.
- The electricians down the wholesalers or pub!
- The internet.
- The library.

As I have been saying throughout, at the end of the day, if you break down each operation into little bite- size pieces then it is not as bad as a lot of people would have you believe. I hope that now you will believe me when I tell you that many of my students say on a Friday afternoon....

"It can't be that easy can it?"
Well now, you know....
"Yes it can!"

This section is a quick look guide to technical jargon that exists within the industry. As usual, I will try to keep explanations short and in layman's terms where possible, if possible!

a.c. (alternating current).
This is what a house is supplied with. The current goes backwards and forwards in the circuit wiring.

Amp.
This is the unit of electrical current. (see current).

Band I circuit.
Any wiring that runs at less than 50V in a house, like phones or burglar alarms.
(see extra low voltage).

Band II circuit.
Any wiring that carries mains voltage.
(see low voltage).

BS 7671.
Code of practice covering the electrical safety of installations. Also known by its traditional name of "The 16th Edition of the regulations".

Cartridge fuse.
A fuse where the fuse wire is inside a ceramic tube. A good example is a plug top fuse or a BS1361 fuse.

Class I Equipment.
Any equipment that is run on mains electricity and needs an earth.

Class II equipment.
Any equipment that is run on mains electricity and does not have an earth.

Class III equipment.
Any equipment, which is supplied via a SELV source and does not have an earth.

Continuity testing.
A test performed on a circuit to make sure the earth reaches the end of it!

Cpc.
(Circuit protective conductor).
The earth wire in a circuit.

Current.
The description of electricity flowing in a circuit. The unit used is amps and the symbol used is I.

d.c. (direct current). — This is what comes from a battery, for instance. The current flows around a circuit in one direction.

Direct contact. — This is getting an electric shock from a live part and expecting it. Perhaps opening a fuse box and sticking your finger in!

Earth fault loop impedance. — This is the impedance of the live-earth circuit from a house back to the supply sub-station. It is expressed in ohms.

Earthing conductor. — This cable is the last path out of a house for fault current. It connects the system earth to the main earthing terminal.

Earth electrode. — This is a rod which is driven into the ground to earth an unearthed house. Used on the T-T earthing system.

Earth fault. — A short circuit between live and earth.

Earthing System. — This is a description of how a house is earthed back to the local sub-station.

EBADS. — (Earthed equipotential bonding and automatic disconnection of supply). This is the standard system of indirect contact protection in a house; it literally means "earth wires and fuses".

Electrical installation Certificate (EIC). — The document that must be issued with a new circuit or installation.

Electrical separation. — Equipment that is electrically isolated from earth. The only example in a house would be a shaver socket.

Exposed conductive part. — This is a part of an electrical installation that you can touch and is made from metal. A chrome lounge dimmer perhaps.

Extra low voltage. — Any voltage in a house up to 50V (see band I circuits).

Extraneous conductive part. — This is a metal part that has nothing to do with and is "extra" to the electrical installation. A gas pipe is a good example.

Fault current. — This is a current that makes a fuse go bang!

Frequency.

(See a.c.) This states what the rate of the current going backwards is and forwards in an a.c. supply and is per second. The unit is "Hertz". A house is supplied with a 50Hz supply, so the current goes in and out of the property 50 times a second.

Impedance.

Opposition to current flow in an a.c. circuit. Unit used is Ohms and the symbol used is Ω. (see a.c. and frequency).

Indirect Contact.

This is receiving a shock off something that is not supposed to live, but becomes live in the event of a fault. (see EEBADS).

Insulation resistance test.

A "pressure" test performed on wiring to make sure it does not "leak" electricity.

IP rating.

A rating given an enclosure to describe its resistance to solids and water intrusion. It is expressed in numbers.

LABC.

(Local authority building control) The people who deal with Part P and all other building regulations to make sure a job complies with current standards.

Live part.

This is any part that carries electricity and by convention includes a neutral conductor.

Low voltage.

Any voltage in a house above 50V. (See band II circuits).

Main equipotential bonding conductor.

An earth cable that is run to the main incomer of any service to a house. Usually gas and water on a house.

Mcb.

(Miniature circuit breaker). Fitted for overload and fault protection. It is a modern version of a fuse.

Megger.

Slang term for an insulation resistance tester.

Minor works certificate.

This is the document that must be issued if an existing circuit is worked on.

Multi-function tester.	This is a combined instrument that can perform all the required tests on an installation. Also known nowadays as a "Part P tester" or "16th Edition tester".
Ohm.	The unit of electrical impedance or resistance. The symbol used is Ω.
OSG.	(On-site guide) A book which explains how BS 7671 works in regard to smaller installations.
Overload current.	This is an overcurrent occurring in a healthy circuit. An example would be too much plugged in to a kitchen ring and the mcb tripping.
pme.	(Protective multiple earth). An earthing system used by suppliers to combine the neutral and earth of the supply. Now known as TN-C-S (see earthing systems).
Polarity testing.	A test to prove that a fuse or light switch is fitted correctly in the live wire of a circuit.
Prospective fault current.	A measurement made to simulate the largest fault current that would flow in the event of a short circuit at the mains position.
Resistance.	The opposition to current flow in a d.c. circuit. The unit used is Ohms and the symbol used is Ω.
Rewireable fuse.	This fuse has an open wire that you can see. It is given the official name of BS3036.
Ring circuit testing.	A special three part test to prove that a ring circuit really is a true ring.
RCBO.	(Residual current breaker with overload). Simply an RCD and MCB combined into one unit.
RCD.	(Residual current device). A unit that monitors a circuit and trips if it detects a very small current leaking away to earth.

I-ON

Safe zone.

A slang term for an area of a wall where the concealed wiring can be less than 50mm from the surface and *not need* mechanical protection.

SELV. (Separated extra low voltage)

A supply that is electrically separated from earth and also extra-low voltage.
An example could be a bell chime transformer.

Short-circuit.

A fault occurring between live and neutral.

Spur.

A wire connected into a ring circuit.

Supplementary equipotential bonding conductor.

This is an earthing cable, primarily used in a bathroom on domestic jobs to comply with "special locations" regulations.
It is *supplementary* to the main bonding.

Volt.

Unit of electrical "pressure" Unit used is V.

Watt.

Unit of electrical power. Symbol used is W.

Ze.

Earth loop impedance external to a house.

Zs.

Earth loop impedance at the end of a circuit.

Numbering indices used in electrical publications:

Milli or m.

One thousandth of a unit.
For instance, a 30mA rcd trip is thirty thousandths of one amp or 0.03A.

Kilo or k.

A thousand of one unit.
For instance, a fault current of 2kA is two thousand amps or 2000A.

Mega or M.

One million of a unit.
For instance, the minimum insulation resistance is 0.5 MΩ.
This could be expressed as a half a million ohms or 500,000Ω.

Giga or G.

One thousand million of a unit.
Some insulation testers now read a maximum of 1GΩ.
This could be expressed as one thousand million ohms or 1,000,000,000Ω.
A very big number indeed!

In December 2006 the IEE and BSI published a proposed new version of the current electrical regulations. This was published as a draft for public comment. The consultation period closed at the end of February 2007. The earliest proposed date for this publication to come into force is the 1st January 2008. If this launch date materializes the old and new regulations are to run side-by-side till 1st July 2008. From this date, the current book will cease to be valid and the new regulations will come into force.

The new 17th Edition regulations have been long awaited and many rumours had circulated prior to the public draft comment document. Now the book has dropped onto my desk I can inform you that your work, will in future years, become easier than it is now! The regulations people have an ongoing obligation to gradually merge our regulations into a "pan-European model". This new book is basically a continuation of that long process. Now if you are new to wiring terminology I suggest you read this book first and come back to this last. However, if you are up to speed with electrical talk then read on. I shall list the changes I have spotted thus far:

- Direct contact has been replaced with "basic contact".
  Same thing as before but with a different name!

- Indirect contact has been replaced by "shock protection" Again, as above, nothing new.

- Five second maximum disconnection now gone.
  Only 0.4s maximum disconnection time is now applicable.

- All circuits going into a bathroom have to be rcd protected.

- Bathroom supplementary equipotential bonding is to be scrapped.

- *All* sockets in a house now have to be rcd protected, not just the ones likely to supply portable equipment outdoors.

- If rcd protected, wiring can now be run outside the "safe zones" of walls without additional mechanical protection.

- All earth loop impedances now based on 230V instead of 240V, so maximum Zs figures are now lower.

- If a bathroom is big enough, socket outlets are now allowed, if more than 3m from the bath.

I am sure others will come to light. Also remember, this is only a draft document, at present, and nothing is "written in stone" just yet. On the whole the up coming publication seems to me to be a retrograde step using the rcd to cure all ills. I am sure, that in the years to come electricians will look back fondly to a time when things were done slightly differently!

I-ON

I-ON

149

I-ON

150